the book of mindful origami

the book of
mindful origami

fold paper, unfold your mind

Samuel Tsang

yellow kite

'If yoga is origami for the body, origami is yoga for the mind.'

Samuel Tsang

Samuel Tsang is a London-based origami teacher. He has been folding origami since he was a child and teaching professionally since 2003. During that time Sam has introduced origami to thousands of students at public and corporate team-building workshops, working with over 100 companies. Sam also helped organise the Guinness World Record for the largest display of origami elephants, which is now permanently displayed at ZSL Whipsnade Zoo.

Sam creates beautiful bespoke origami bouquets and undertakes commissions for private individuals and businesses. He also runs a monthly origami workshop open to beginners and experienced folders at the Queen of Hoxton club in East London. All details are available on his website, www.sesames.co.uk

Born in London, Sam was brought up with traditional Chinese values, a mixture of Buddhism, Taoism and Confucianism. He now lives in West London with his wife, two daughters and a house full of origami.

www.mindfulorigami.com
@mindfulorigami #mindfulorigami

www.mindFOLDness.com
@mindFOLDness #mindFOLDness

bases

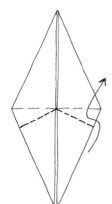

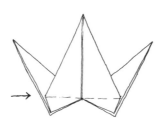

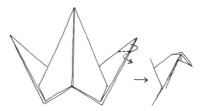

simple traditional models

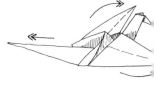

advanced models

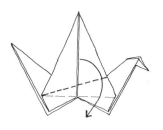

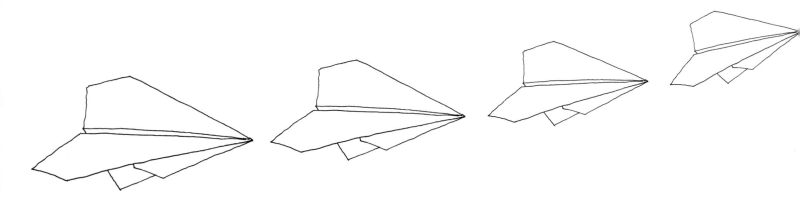

the book of mindful origami

introduction

Most of us encounter origami as a child. Maybe it was on a lazy afternoon when a parent picked up a piece of paper, folded it into an aeroplane and threw it across the room? Or perhaps it was in the school playground when a friend ran up to you with a fortune teller, asked you to pick a number then a colour, opened a flap and revealed the name of a secret admirer or your future path in life?

Do you remember the first time you saw an origami model? What was it? Who folded it?

I have been teaching origami for over a decade and over that time many of my students have commented on how they've found origami not only to be fun and relaxing but also therapeutic, with some even comparing it to meditation. Indeed, I have read references of Zen Buddhists using origami as a form of meditation.

Origami requires you to use your hands, eyes and mind and it will help you learn to focus and concentrate.

It will teach you to be methodical, more patient and can help you improve your memory and hand–eye coordination. In short, origami is a path to mindfulness, or as I like to call it, mindFOLDness®.

Many people are apprehensive about trying origami – the models look complicated so naturally they associate it with difficulty. In reality if you can fold a piece of paper in half you can do origami.

It's so easy – children love it – and indeed, origami is a perfect activity to do with children and it is used in many schools to teach fractions and geometry. There are also therapists using origami as an aid to help children with developmental issues. In this book, I hope to share the fun and magic of origami with you, and inspire you with the creative and thoughtful process of turning a flat piece of paper into a beautiful piece of art.

origami: the art of folding paper

Origami is the Japanese name for the art of folding paper. Although today origami is most commonly associated with Japan, it is thought that paper folding came to life in different guises in China, Europe and Japan.

Paper was invented in China around 100BC, so it is likely the practice began here, but initially paper was expensive to make and reserved for official and religious ceremonies. Early examples of origami can be seen at traditional Chinese funerals. Paper 'spirit' money was burnt for the deceased to be used in the afterlife. Often the pieces of paper were folded into the shape of a traditional Chinese gold nugget and this tradition is still practised.

It was in Japan that origami grew into the art form that we know today. It is believed that in 6BC Buddhist monks took paper to Japan, where it was used in religious ceremonies. Shinto priests used a ceremonial wand called a 'shide' that was made from folded strips of paper. Initially paper was a rare commodity and origami was reserved for ceremonial purposes: origami butterflies were used to decorate sake bottles during Japanese weddings, for example. As the process of making paper became more industrialised it became cheaper and more widely available, used for printing books and teaching children to read and write.

It is not known how origami originated but I like to think that it was a child who first discovered that they could fold paper from their school textbook into a bird or butterfly. Before the printed press origami models were handed down from parent to child.

The first reference to origami in print was in the eighteenth century – in the origami book *Hiden Senbazuru Orikata (The Secret of Folding One Thousand Cranes)*, published in 1797. But origami only started to become a popular hobby outside of Japan in the twentieth century. In 1954 a Japanese origamist named Akira Yoshizawa created a set of instructional diagrams using arrows and dotted lines to denote the different folds required to create a model. This instruction set has now become the standard in all origami books.

With the advent of the computer in the 1970s some mathematicians and scientists started to study the mathematical principles behind origami. Like a lot of scientific research, what was done out of academic curiosity has led to some unexpected uses. They discovered that the principles behind origami could be used to fold large objects into smaller, more compact shapes and this knowledge has since been used in satellite solar panelling, car air bags and medical heart stents.

The number of unique traditional origami models is actually quite limited, numbering fewer than 100 but in the last two decades the number of origami designs has exploded with the creation of computer programs that can actually create new origami designs. The popularity of origami is still growing every year.

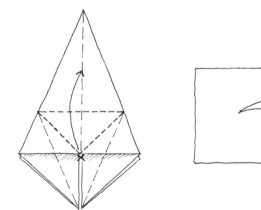

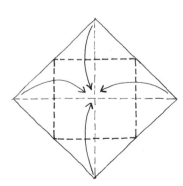

perspective, persistence, patience and practice

I have taught origami to complete beginners for over 10 years now. When I first started teaching workshops I would sometimes encounter individuals who became frustrated with origami. I even had a couple of people walk out of a workshop because they had become so exasperated with it. I wondered what had caused these individuals to have what, in my mind, was quite an extreme reaction. After all, for most people, origami is an inconsequential skill. I thought about these people and I came to the conclusion that they were frustrated because they were not understanding the instructions I was giving them, and I believed that this was a failing in my teaching skills and ability to convey the instructions simply enough for everyone to understand. This was what was causing them to be unsatisfied and unfulfilled by their experience of origami and ultimately to give up.

The problem with that conclusion is that in a class of 40 or 50 people of all ages, backgrounds and abilities the majority grasped the concept and successfully completed the models. Even more importantly, there were other individuals who also failed to complete the model yet did not leave or seem to get even slightly frustrated.

I pondered this for a long time until I decided to ask one individual why they were getting frustrated. Their response was, 'I feel stupid that I can't grasp such a simple skill.'

One of the greatest problems with our generation is our belief that we should be able to grasp any concept or skill on our first try, so failure to be able to do this, in turn, makes us a failure. Is it reasonable or rational to believe that we should be able to understand every concept or grasp a new skill on our first exposure to it?

If you find that you are unable to do something the first time, all it means is that your mind has never encountered that problem before and as such you have not learned the skills to deal with it.

This may seem like cold comfort for some but even the simplest skills such as reading and writing take us years of practice to perfect.

Origami seems simple. Its primary skill is the ability to fold a piece of paper in half. But in the same sense the fundamental skill of being a concert pianist is the ability to press a piano key. It would, of course, be absurd to think that after just one piano lesson you could replicate the performance of a concert pianist. You realise that to be a proficient pianist requires more than to be able to press a piano key, it requires the knowledge and skill to read music, to have the hand–eye coordination to play, and it takes countless months of practice to become even mildly proficient at the piano let alone be a concert pianist. The same is true for origami. The fundamental skill is to be able to fold paper but you also need to learn to read and understand the instructions, have hand–eye coordination, spatial reasoning to know where to make folds, and enough practice to be able to make the fold with precision and accuracy.

The models in this book are split into different levels of difficulty. You should be able to complete the simplest models on the first or second try. The intermediate models might take you three or four attempts and the advanced models might take you many more (the most difficult model – the squirrel – is for people who are very experienced in origami and could take months for you to learn).

The models gradually get more difficult as you progress through the book and you should view origami as a puzzle, something that you may not be able to solve on the first, second or even the tenth try. But as with a puzzle there is immense satisfaction when you crack it! So when you are stuck, remember that failure to complete a model does not make you a failure, it just means you have not practised enough. If you find you get frustrated while folding, put the model away and come back to it later, maybe even weeks later. If you are still really stuck and want more immediate help to avoid further frustration, you can go to the mindful origami website (www.mindfulorigami. com) where there are videos to help you. So, I will leave you with my four P's for mindful origami (these are also valid for life in general!):

perspective – don't take it too seriously.

persistence – you only fail when you give up.

patience – any skill will take time to learn.

practice – only with continuous practice will you become proficient.

the path to mindfulness

In today's world, we live in a relentless 'rushed' state. From the moment we wake we hurry to get to work, swallow our lunch to get back to our desks, and power through our tasks to meet our deadlines. We work long hours, multitask each day and respond to a constant stream of queries using multiple devices.

When we are constantly rushed, our bodies become tired. When our minds are rushed, we become forgetful, unsure and anxious. We are constantly trying to reach the next checkpoint and we are rarely able to appreciate the present moment.

The accepted definition of mindfulness is to be aware of the present moment without judgement. To be mindful is simply to be conscious and truly aware of your own thoughts, feelings and surroundings.

It has also been described as the process of quieting the mind to free it of distracting thoughts, or as the opposite of 'multitasking' – focusing your mind on the current thought or activity you are engaged in.

We are often so busy trying to complete the next task that we forget to enjoy what we are doing in the present. By living in the present moment you can start to appreciate and enjoy the life you are living and be free of stress, anxiety and fear. By learning to be mindful it will help you to stop negative thoughts, reduce your stress and anxieties. Indeed, mindfulness training has now been recognised by the National Health Service in the UK as a way to reduce stress and anxiety and promote mental well-being.

Mindfulness is not happiness but it is directly connected to it. It is not a quick fix to all the problems in your life, it is not even a slow fix, it is just a signpost indicating a possible pathway to happiness.

Being mindful is to know where you are right now, but it is up to you to find the correct path to where you want to be. Mindfulness is the compass or map; you still have to climb those mountains yourself.

There is no wrong or right way to practise mindfulness. Being mindful is not something measurable, it is a process to become aware of your true self. It will help you identify the cause of stress and sadness in your life and once identified you can either try to fix the problem, avoid its causes or learn to manage and accept them.

You will also become aware of what truly makes you happy and not the expectations that have been drummed into you by society.

Two burgeoning trends have struck me over the past decade. The first is the increasing popularity of mindful activities such as yoga, pilates, tai chi and meditation. The second has been the huge resurgence in arts and crafts. I believe that both are a direct response to people needing to calm their minds and slow their lives. Many of us have office jobs where we sit in front of a computer screen all day. We tap away at a keyboard, creating documents and spreadsheets that might be looked at once and never seen again. In the digital world, our work is virtual – fleeting – and we are often just a small cog in a big machine. We can rarely see the physical fruits of our labour. All this has led to a desire, a need even, for a creative outlet; we want to be able to make something real, something we can touch. Origami is a fusing of both these needs: creating some calm and producing something tangible. When you are learning to fold, your hands, eyes and mind are fully focused on the task of creation and you are able to ignore external distractions. Through origami you can find calm and be in the moment.

'There is more to life than increasing its speed.'
Gandhi

mindful origami

Origami is simply the act of folding paper, but it is the intent and thought behind this action that determines whether it is positive or negative and therefore whether it is mindful or not. Any activity can be done mindfully and this is the ultimate goal – to be mindful at all times; to be aware and enjoy your life.

Mindful origami uses the creative process of folding a model as a meditative aid and the models you make are a physical manifestation of your desire to be more mindful and hopefully happier.

In practising mindful origami it is important to remember that the meditation and the learning process are more important than completing the origami model. Your intent should be to meditate on a theme and to learn the process of origami. Completion of a model is just an aid in the process. It is a piece of folded paper; there are no consequences if you do not complete the model.

There are two stages to becoming mindful during your origami practice. The first stage is to slip into a calm frame of mind, where your attention is focused on the piece of paper in your hands. During this phase you will not be meditating but you will be concentrating and learning. When you are in learning mode your mind is focusing on the present moment and will naturally block out all distracting thoughts.

The second stage of mindful origami is the meditation. I have folded tens of thousands of models and there are some models that I can fold without thinking. When I am crafting these models I am calm and can allow my thoughts to wander. Sometimes my mind will start to crystallise a thought or recall a memory, person or feeling associated with the model. When you have learned to fold your model by heart, without referring to the illustrations, you will be able to reflect on its meaning – or theme – and its effect or presence in your own life. For instance whenever I fold an origami crane I think of the story of Sadako Sasaki (see page 84), while other models make me think of important events in my own life. I designed an origami rose for my wife and named it the Carmen Curler rose (Curler is the method by which the rose is created – it is curled). Now, whenever I fold this flower, I think of Carmen and reflect on our life together. I have also designed a turtle and a squirrel for my two daughters, Cammy and Remy (see page 101 for how to fold your own squirrel; the turtle is a little complicated for beginners so doesn't feature in this book). These models have become a focal point or a 'totem' for my thoughts about each person in my family. They take just a few minutes to complete and during that time I think about that person only.

Like yoga and pilates, where the more advanced poses take time to learn and you may not manage them on the first attempt, so it is with the origami models you will be folding. When you look at your model do not judge it or judge yourself, there is no perfection. If you are stuck on a difficult step, do not be frustrated. Take a breath and try again. If the model doesn't look like the picture, do not be upset; no two flowers are identical. The learning is all part of the process of becoming mindful. And like yoga or meditation the benefits of origami only become apparent if you practise regularly. As you become more accomplished and proficient at folding, you will soon be able to enter a mindful state as you create your models. While meditating you may not crystallise any thoughts or draw any conclusions; true understanding takes time and effort. Through repeated practice you will learn to perfect the model and once you have, you will be able to focus your mind on the meditation and eventually come to a conclusion.

'The more you meditate upon good thoughts; the better will be your world and the world at large.'
Confuscius

about this book

In this book I have chosen 16 origami models for you to work through: 12 traditional models and four of my own design (the kite and the final three). The models start from the simplest and progressively become more challenging. I suggest you work methodically through the book from start to finish. If you are new to origami do not attempt the hardest models first as this will just frustrate you. You must learn to walk before you can run.

Work calmly and steadily through each step. Check the step you have just done before moving on. As you fold, study the paper, the lines and the colours. Feel the texture of the paper between your fingers and notice the sound as you make each crease.

Each model within the book has a suggested theme to reflect on. Try to relate each model to an associated thought, memory or feeling, though note that the themes are merely my suggestion so allow your thoughts to drift and wander; mindful origami is an exploration of your own meditations and feelings. If you find that something is consuming your attention, stop folding and let it take its natural progression through your mind. Once that thought or feeling has subsided, continue with your origami.

When you complete the model reflect on what thoughts and feelings you had while folding. You can write them down in the space at the end of each chapter to build up a log of your meditations or, if you have crystallised a particular thought, aim or idea, write it on the actual model itself and hang it somewhere prominent. By placing the models somewhere you can see them every day they will act as visual reminders of your intentions. I would also encourage you to offer your models to others. Give them freely to people you know as well as to complete strangers without expecting anything in return. Think of this as a mindful act: making others happy with a small gesture of kindness.

Finally, be kind to yourself. The majority of models within this book are for complete beginners and will not take long to grasp; the last few are more complicated. If you find you are stuck on a particular step, stop folding, but continue meditating on the theme and topic. When you are ready, pick up the model and slowly turn the model, noting the position of each crease and edge. Read the step you are stuck on and try again. Remember, the learning is just as mindful as the folding.

paper

Origami can be folded from any paper available. The vast majority of origami is folded from square paper but there are many examples of it being folded from rectangular, pentagonal, hexagonal and octagonal shaped paper. The first model in this book, for example, is an envelope and can be folded from a standard A4 sheet. On page 31 there are instructions on how to cut out a square from a rectangle and you should do this for the house, tree, fortune teller and windmill models. For the remaining 11 models there are pull-out pages at the back of the book. These pages have crease patterns printed on them, which show where all the fold lines are on each model. By using these crease patterns and following the instructions in the book you should be able to complete the models more easily.

The crease patterns give you another outlet for artistic expression: colour them in and see what your subconscious reveals. There is also a mystery crease pattern – fold it and try to figure out what it is. You can also print additional crease patterns by visiting www.mindfulorigami.com and downloading the free pdf files.

Origami paper can also be found in most art stores and online. It comes in many sizes, colours and textures. The smallest origami crane models measure 0.1mm and have to be viewed under a microscope, while the largest is the size of a football field. The most common origami paper size is 15 x 15cm and this format comes in the largest range of patterns, colours and textures. This is the most popular size as it is the most easily manipulated and folded – not so small that it becomes difficult to fold by adults and not too large so that it becomes unwieldy to fold.

The paper weight and thickness is usually between 60 and 80gsm but any paper can be folded as long as it can hold a crease (though I do not recommend folding paper that is thicker than 140gsm as it is difficult to crease due to its stiffness and also the paper tends to rip along the fold lines).

If you are new to origami then you can just use standard A4 paper and cut it into a square to fold. Then after you have mastered a few of the basic models why not treat yourself and purchase some traditional coloured origami papers.

14 steps to mindFOLDness®

1   Wash your hands. You can consider this a cleansing ritual but in reality it is just to avoid leaving greasy fingerprints on your finished model.

2   Sit in a comfortable and quiet place with a table. Relax your body and clear your mind of the daily grind.

3   Read the instructions for each model thoroughly before beginning to fold.

4   Think about the theme of the story. Close your eyes if it helps. Try to recall a memory of your own that relates to the theme.

5   Fold when you are ready, following each step carefully.

6   Meditate. Let your thoughts drift and wander.

7   Consciously use your senses while folding. See the lines and shadows, feel the texture of the paper, hear the sounds as you fold.

8   Stop and take a breather to check you have folded each step correctly.

9   Continue folding until the model is complete.

10   Now pick up the model and appreciate what you have created. Well done!

11   Each time you fold and meditate keep a log of your thoughts and feelings in the space at the end of each chapter. If along the way you have crystallised any thoughts, write them on the model itself.

12   Place or hang the model somewhere prominent. Whenever you look at this model you will associate it with that thought or memory.

13   Repeat the model until you can make it by heart and then you will be able to purely focus on the meditation.

14   Carry out mindful acts of kindness by giving away your completed models without expecting anything in return.

instruction symbols: dashes, dots and arrows

Set out in this section are the basic instruction symbols for the folds used throughout the book. If you're new to origami, you will need to read and practise each one of these folds before beginning any of the models. Think of them as warm-up exercises.

valley fold

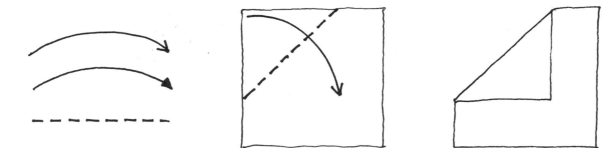

This is the most basic origami fold, represented by a dash line and an arrow to indicate the direction of the fold. Fold the paper towards you and crease along the line. If you look at the crease sideways it will look like an upside-down 'V'.

mountain fold

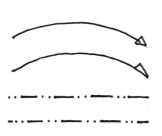 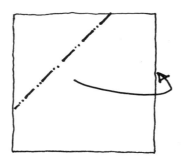 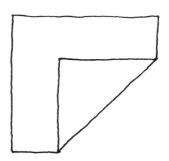

A mountain fold is indicated by a dash-dot-dot-dash line and an arrow to indicate the direction of the fold. You fold the paper so that it is folded behind itself (or away from you), which creates a crease that looks like the peak of a mountain.

fold and unfold

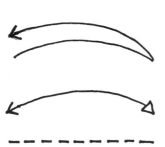 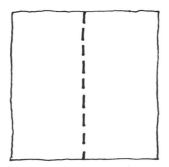 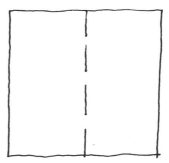

This symbol means that the paper is folded in half, then unfolded. This results in a crease line that can be used later.

turn over (and an invisible line)

This symbol indicates you have to turn the model over. The dotted line indicates the edge of the paper that is now underneath.

rotate

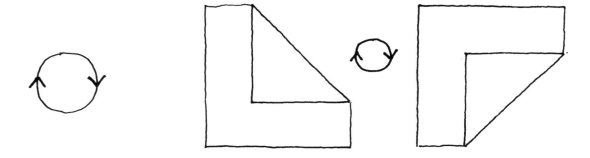

This symbol is the instruction for rotating the paper. The arrow indicates whether to rotate clockwise or anticlockwise and a number in the middle will indicate if you should rotate by 90 or 180 degrees.

inside reverse fold

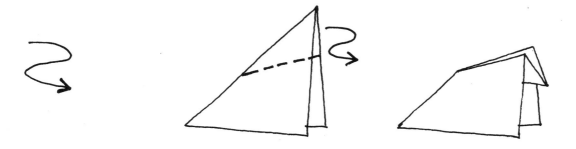

To make an inside reverse fold you have to push a fold in on itself. The easiest way to make an inside reverse fold is to make a valley fold on the dotted line first, then unfold it and push the fold in on itself.

outside reverse fold

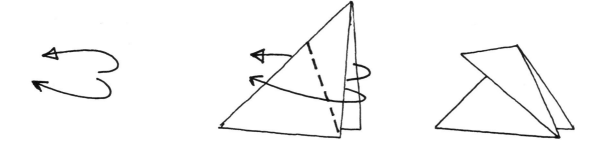

To make an outside reverse fold you have to pull the two edges indicated over the paper. Imagine it as if you were pulling the hood of your raincoat over your head. As with an inside reverse fold, the easiest way to make an outside reverse fold is to make a valley fold on the dotted line, then unfold it and use the crease to make the outside fold.

fold point to point

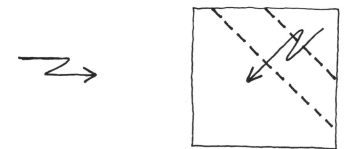 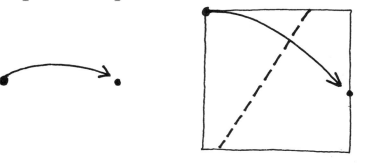 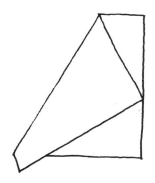

This symbol means that you should fold along the dotted line so that the two points indicated lie on top of each other.

pleat (or accordion) fold

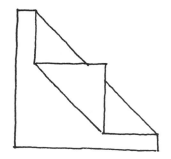

As it sounds, a pleat, or accordion, fold indicates that you need to make two folds. The first is a valley fold and the second a mountain fold so that you end up with a pleat as shown.

open

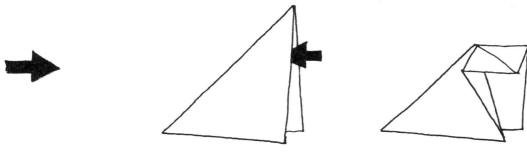

An arrow like this means that you need to open out the model by separating the two edges of the paper where indicated. Usually when you see this symbol there are some pre-made creases on the model that will cause it to open along natural lines and hold its shape.

pull

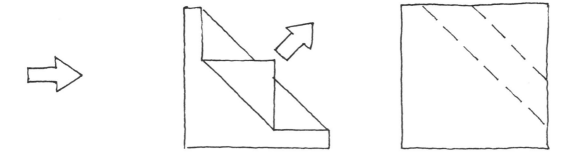

Simply pull at the point indicated.

inside crimp

 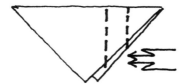 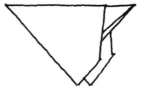

This symbol indicates that you have to make folds through both layers and then you have to sink one fold inside the other. Another way to explain it would be to make an inside reverse fold and then another inside reverse fold in the other direction. Essentially, you are pleating the section indicated.

outside crimp

 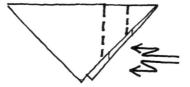 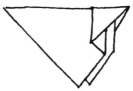

An inside crimp in reverse, so an outside reverse fold and then another outside reverse fold in the other direction. Again, you have to make folds through both layers.

sink

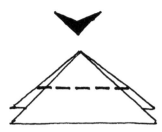

A sink fold tucks part of a model inside the other. The easiest way to make sink folds is to fold and unfold right through all the layers on the dotted line, then gently tuck the point indicated down into the section inside.

inflate

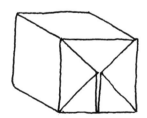

This symbol means you have to blow into the hole to inflate the model. Before inflating, make sure you have a dry mouth so you don't wet and damage your model. Also don't hold the model too tightly when blowing as this will prevent it from inflating fully.

bases

The 'bases' provided in this section are the most basic form of origami and the starting point for a vast number of models. Think of them as the foundation of the model you are folding. By learning to fold these bases correctly and accurately you will enable yourself to fold complex models without frustration. If the base is not accurate then later fold lines and edges will be out of alignment and you will find it difficult to complete the model. You must learn to walk before you can run so as with the instruction symbols, do please practise all these bases before starting any of the models.

make a square from rectangular paper

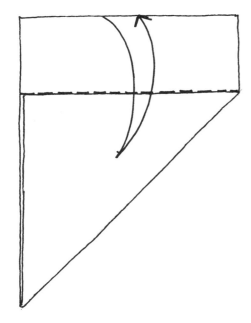

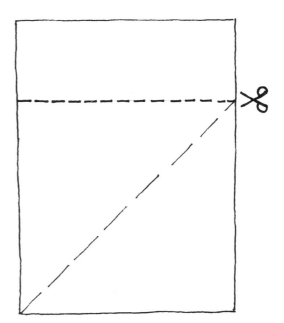

step 1

Valley fold and unfold along the dotted line – the
bottom right corner should meet the left edge.

step 2

Cut along the small dotted line and you will have
a perfect square.

square base

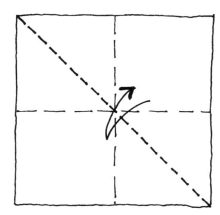

step 2

Fold and unfold along one of the diagonals. Make the fold from corner to corner trying to be as neat and accurate as possible.

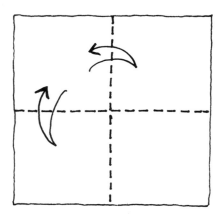

step 1

First you will need to fold some squares. Start with the white side of the paper facing you. Fold and unfold along the horizontal and vertical dotted lines.

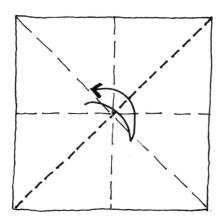

step 3

Turn the paper over so that the coloured side is facing you. Fold and unfold the other diagonal, again corner to corner.

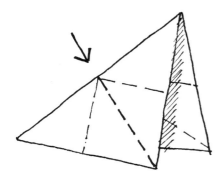

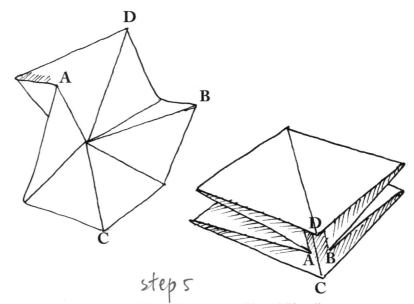

step 4

Turn it back over to the white side. The model should stand up like a wigwam. You are now going to pack away the wigwam by collapsing it. Push down on the centre point as indicated to begin to flatten the model.

step 5

Two of the corners (A and B) will start to pop up – bring them together. Then bring the other two corners (C and D) together and the whole model will collapse down into the square base.

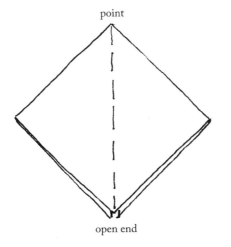

point

open end

The vast majority of basic origami models begin with the square or the triangle base (see page 34) so I would urge you to become familiar with this base before progressing to the models. Note that it has a point and open end. Also note that it has four branches. Origami is all about symmetry and whatever fold you make on one branch will normally have to be repeated on the three other branches.

triangle base

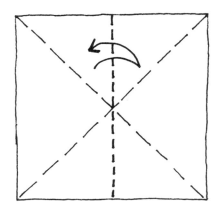

step 2

Valley fold and unfold along the vertical line.

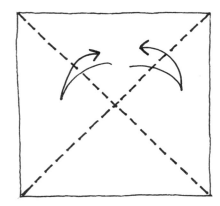

step 1

Start with the white side of the paper facing you.
Valley fold both diagonals, corner to corner.

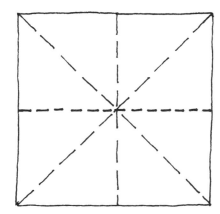

step 3

Turn the paper over on to the coloured side and
valley fold along the horizontal line.

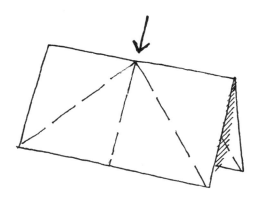

step 4

Turn the model back over on to the white side; it should stand up like a tent. You are now going to pack your tent away by collapsing it. Push down on the point as indicated to begin to flatten it.

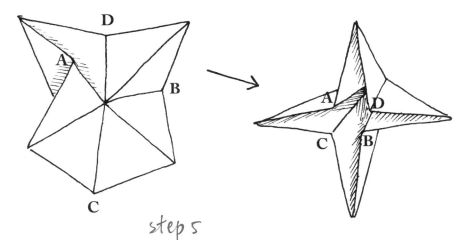

step 5

As you push down, bring points A and B together. Then bring C and D together. Flatten the model and it will collapse into the triangle base.

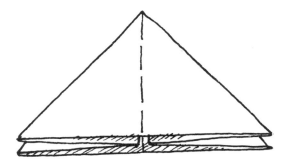

Become familiar with this base before progressing to the models.

bird base

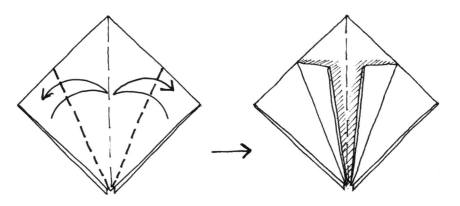

step 1

Start by folding a square base (see page 32).
Valley fold the two upper layers then unfold.

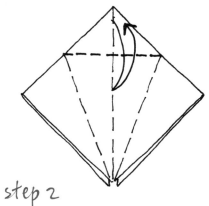

step 2

Valley fold the top triangle down.

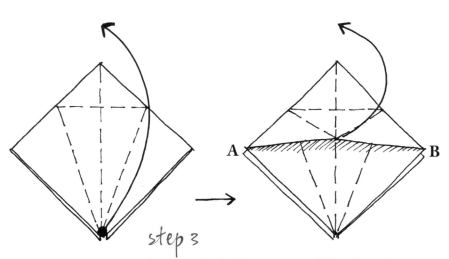

step 3

Valley fold only the upper layer lifting from the
point indicated. As you lift, it will pivot along the
dotted line and points A and B will move towards
each other.

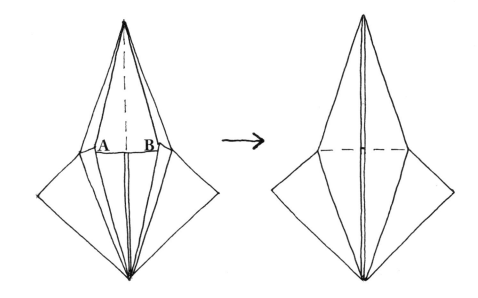

step 4

Push points A and B down towards the centre line and flatten the model. Then turn over and repeat steps 1–4 on the other side. You will end up with a flat diamond shape. Steps 3 and 4 are also known as a petal fold.

This is called a bird base because it is the starting point for many bird models. If you look at it from the side, you will see it has a triangle hump in the middle which is the body of the bird. It has two parallel wings and what look like two legs which often become the head and the tail of the bird.

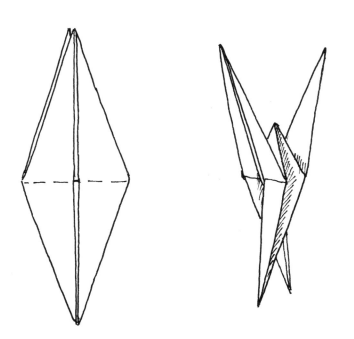

fish base

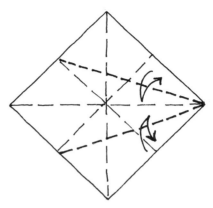

step 2

Valley fold and unfold along the small dotted lines.

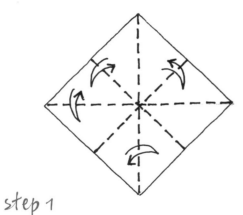

step 1

Valley fold and unfold along each dotted line.

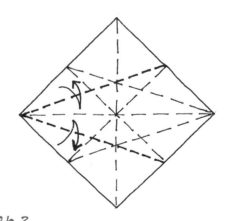

step 3

Valley fold and unfold along the small dotted lines.

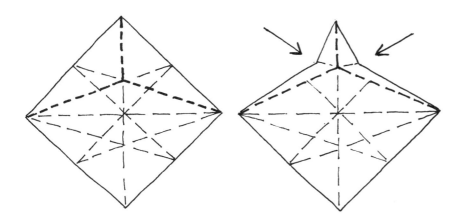
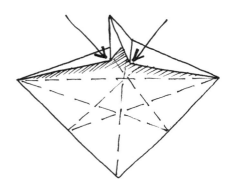

step 4

Valley fold on the dotted lines. As you fold, push down on the edges where indicated to flatten the model.

step 5

Push down at the points indicated – the edges will flatten and you will form a triangular fin. Now repeat the last two steps on the bottom half.

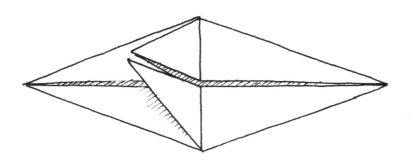

This is called a fish base because it is the starting point for many fish models. You will notice it has two triangle flaps on each side that can be used as fins.

Please note that the bird and fish bases are just the recognised names given to them by the origami community. Any base can be folded into infinite shapes, objects and animals, for instance in this book the fish base is the starting point for folding an elephant (see page 94). Of course, if you look back far enough in the fossil record you will find that the elephant did indeed have aquatic ancestors...

'Kindness is its own reward.'
Proverbs 11:17

envelope 信 封

Think of the last time you heard the snap of your letterbox as an envelope fell to the floor. Most likely you turned away with indifference, instinctively assuming that the folded paper case harboured a bill? But the humble envelope was not born a carrier of demands; it actually started life as a bearer of gifts. Invented in China, the envelope was originally used to wrap gifts of money for court officials, a symbolic tradition that is still observed in China over New Year. To celebrate the beginning of each year adults offer little red envelopes filled with money to the younger generation. And as a mark of a celebration, the same red envelopes are also given on birthdays, graduations and weddings.

As you crease your paper, meditate on the kindness in the act of giving to another person. Kindness can be anything, from donating money to charity to offering your seat to someone on a train that needed it more than you. Now think about when you have been the recipient of an act of kindness. Contemplate that act of kindness, and the thoughts and feelings behind being the giver and receiver.

reflections

For my wife's birthday one year I made a large jigsaw puzzle of our first photo together.
I wrapped each jigsaw puzzle piece in one of these envelopes and hid them all around the house. Each envelope had a clue pointing to the next. She spent two days trying to solve each clue and hunting all the pieces for the jigsaw. Her smile told me it was worth the wait.

For this model you will need a rectangular piece of paper – an A4 sheet is perfect.

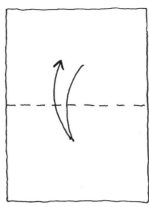

step 1

Valley fold and unfold along the dotted line.

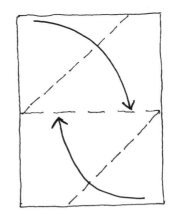

step 2

Valley fold along each dotted line; the opposing corners will meet along the central crease line.

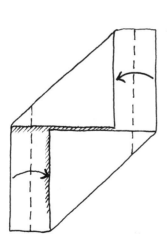

step 3

Valley fold along each dotted line.

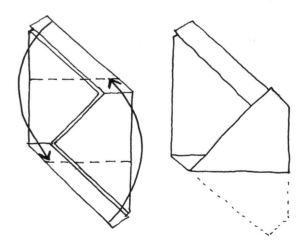

step 4

Turn the model anticlockwise by 45 degrees and valley fold along the dotted lines.

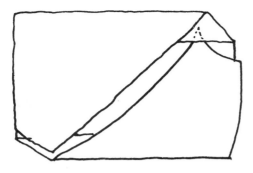

step 5

Slide the right-hand flap into the pocket at the top, then do the same with the left-hand flap.

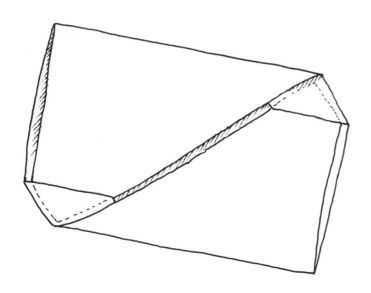

who was the last person that was kind to you?

In this age of instant digital communication a real letter can still offer so much pleasure. After you complete this envelope, send it to someone. Write them a thank you letter and fold your letter to become this envelope. The two clipped corners seal your envelope so it's ready to post.

Note down your reflections as you fold.

....

....

....

....

....

....

....

'Home is where the heart is.'
Pliny the Elder

house 房子

What is a home? Is it a house? A town? A country? Or is it simply where we feel safe or where we find our loved ones? Our home is not necessarily a building; it can be anywhere – a river or mountain, a library, a church or a quiet spot in the garden.

Contemplate what your home means to you. Where do you feel the safest and most at ease? Maybe you are there now, reading this book. Think about the peace and calm that sanctuary gives you. Appreciate the moment; the warmth and feeling of home. What is it about your home that makes you feel this peace? Is it the memories of the place or the people that live there?

When our home is clean and uncluttered we can feel relaxed and unburdened. The same is true for our minds; we all carry unnecessary baggage there. But on the path to mindfulness we must learn to think clearly. We must declutter our lives and our minds. Think about which things are important: throw away the useless and unnecessary possessions in your life and at the same time clear your mind of negative thoughts and memories.

reflections

Moving home is one of the most stressful things in life and in the last decade I have moved house three times. Yet each time the struggles of the move are short and the move always represents a new beginning and new hope for the future. Despite my initial hesitation or reluctance, with each move my life became happier. During each move I was able to reduce the amount of unnecessary possessions I owned. A lot of the useless and pointless things I had collected over the years were sold, donated or simply thrown away. I had fewer possessions after each move but what was left were the important things, the things that had real value in my life – the photos, the letters, the objects that make me smile inside.

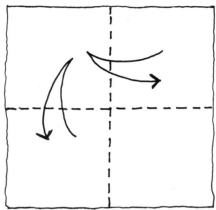

step 1

Valley fold and unfold along the dotted lines.

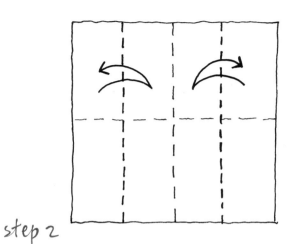

step 2

Valley fold and unfold along each dotted line; the left and right edges will meet along the centre line.

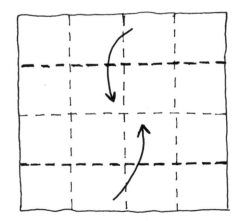

step 3

Valley fold along the dotted lines; the top and bottom edges will meet along the centre line.

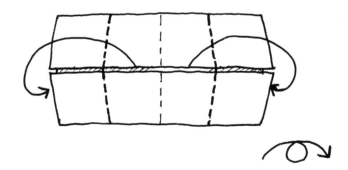

step 4

Mountain fold along the dotted lines; the left and right edges will meet along the centre line on the back. Turn the model over so the folded sections are facing upwards.

step 5

Valley fold and unfold along the dotted lines.

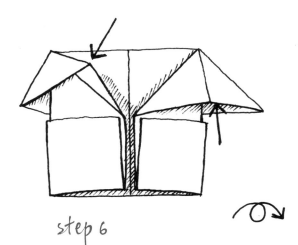

step 6

Open out the flaps you just folded. Push down on the top of each corner and the flap will flatten to form the sloping roof of the house. Turn the model over.

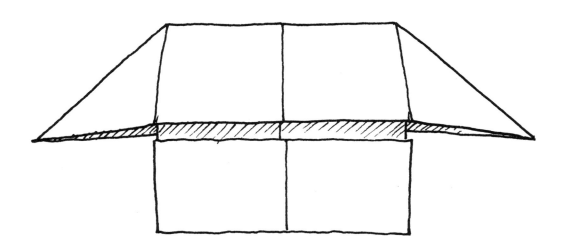

'If you think in terms of a year, plant a seed;
if in terms of ten years, plant trees;
if in terms of 100 years, teach the people.'
Confucius

tree 樹

If you live in the countryside, trees are likely to be such a recurrent part of your environment that you probably don't even notice them; while for those of us living in cities, a flash of greenery amid the concrete landscape can be quite a rarity. Whatever your surroundings, have you ever stopped to think about a tree and the role it plays in our lives? Trees are not only linked to our well-being; they are our life force. They provide us with food in the form of fruits and nuts; wood to use as fuel; building material for our homes; medicine, such as quinine and aspirin; and most importantly the air we breathe – trees are the lungs of our planet. In many cultures trees and forests are so revered, they are held sacred and believed to be the home of spirits and demons.

When you folded your house model you thought about your home. Now I'm going to ask you to expand that meditation to include its surrounding areas. As you crease your tree, contemplate your daily interaction with your environment and your relationship with it. There is no denying that we pollute our planet and in turn affect our well-being. Are there things you could do to make your environment better? Perhaps recycle more? Reduce your usage of water and electricity? Consider your surroundings and whether there is room for nature to be a bigger part of it.

reflections

When we moved into our new home I decided to plant some fruit trees in the garden for my daughters. While planting those trees I hoped they would grow strong alongside my children and imagined they would provide fruit for them as they grew and would one day be big enough to shade them from the summer heat. This world belongs to the next generation and we are all temporary visitors; we should leave the world in a better state than we found it.

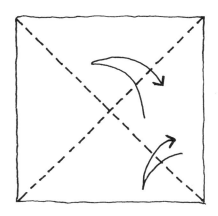

step 1

Valley fold and unfold along the dotted line, then turn the model clockwise by 45 degrees.

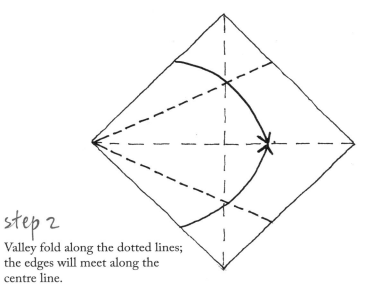

step 2

Valley fold along the dotted lines; the edges will meet along the centre line.

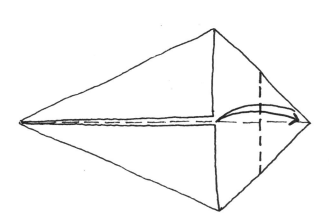

step 3

Valley fold and unfold along the dotted line; the corner will meet the centre line.

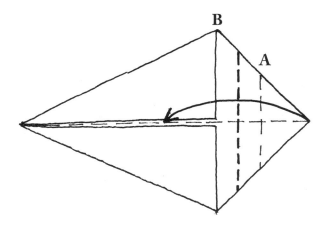

step 4

Valley fold on the dotted lines. The existing crease line A will sit on top of line B.

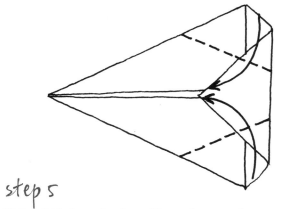

step 5

Valley fold along the dotted lines; the two edges
will meet in the middle.

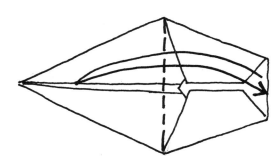

step 6

Valley fold and unfold on the
dotted line.

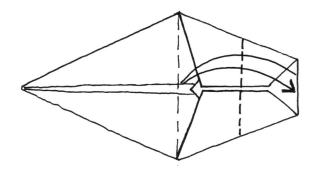

step 7

Valley fold and unfold on the dotted line.

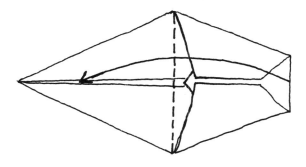

step 8

Valley fold on the dotted line.

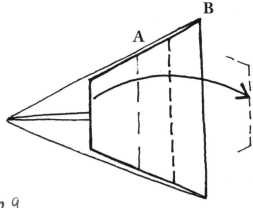

step 9

Valley fold on the dotted line so that the existing crease line A sits on top of line B. Flip the model over and turn it anticlockwise 90 degrees.

Note down your reflections as you fold.

....

....

....

....

....

....

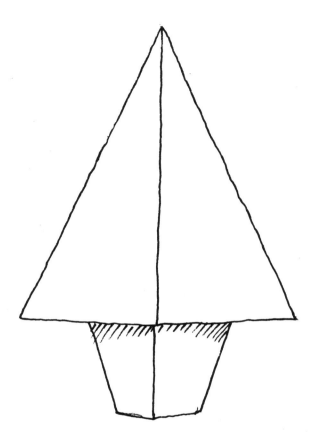

If you fold your tree down the middle slightly it should stand upright.

'Travel is fatal to prejudice, bigotry and narrow-mindedness.'
Mark Twain

plane 飛機

The aeroplane is one of man's greatest inventions. It has transformed the world we live in, allowing us to travel and see its many wonders. With each new destination, we have the opportunity to learn from a different culture; to see through another's eyes and to be challenged by a new philosophy.

When travelling we should allow ourselves to be open-minded. Too often we have preconceived ideas about how things 'should be' and fail to see what is really in front of us and how things actually are. New cultures show us different outlooks and it is inspiring and invigorating to challenge our views of the world.

Sadly, too often we end up in tourist areas that have been packaged and sanitised to fulfil a preconceived image of a place, and bear no semblance to the lives of the local people. Next time you travel why not visit an area that is not in the guidebook? Strike up a conversation with a local if you can, find out where they would go.

As you fold your paper plane, think about the places you have been and the places you would like to go. Recall what you learned on those journeys. Did you start to see the world differently? Perhaps you tasted a food or drink you had never tried before? Or watched a magnificent sunset from a new horizon? Travel should be an opportunity to learn from other cultures and pursue knowledge.

reflections

During an aerodynamics lecture at university a student threw a paper plane. It glided all the way to the front of the hall and landed where the professor, Dr Ranjan Vepa, was teaching. He picked up the model and instantly challenged the class to a paper plane throwing competition. They climbed the stairs to the top of the building and each student folded a paper plane and threw it off the roof. Each plane was timed to see how long it stayed in the air and the professor's plane won by a huge margin. He then told the class to investigate why their plane designs had failed and how they could be improved. The moral of the story is: even something as trivial as a student throwing a paper plane can be turned into an opportunity to acquire knowledge. The second moral is: never challenge an aerodynamics professor to a paper plane throwing competition – you will lose!

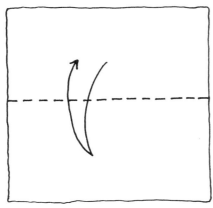

step 1

Valley fold and unfold along the dotted line.

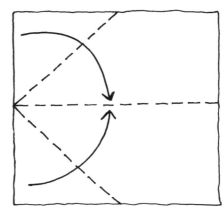

step 2

Valley fold on the dotted lines.

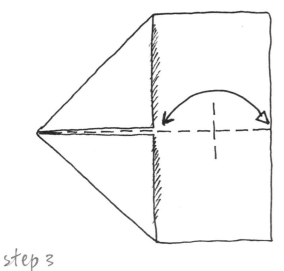

step 3

Vally fold and unfold along the central dotted line,
then just make a small crease along the short line.

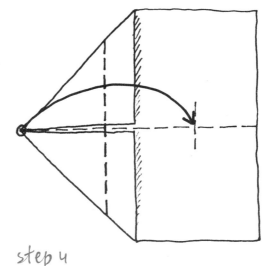

step 4

Fold the tip of the plane in to meet the short crease.

step 5

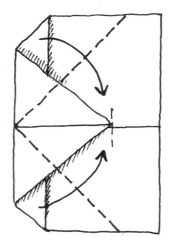

Valley fold along the dotted lines to create the plane's nose.

step 6

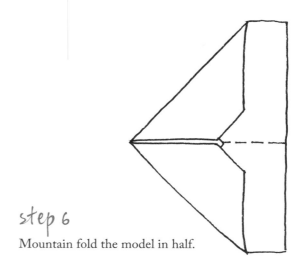

Mountain fold the model in half.

step 7

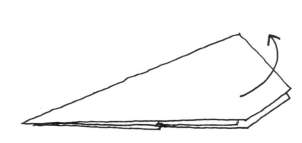

Valley fold along the dotted line so that the upper edge meets the bottom edge. Repeat on the other side.

step 8

Open up the wings on both sides and the plane is completed.

Gently throw the plane and it will fly.

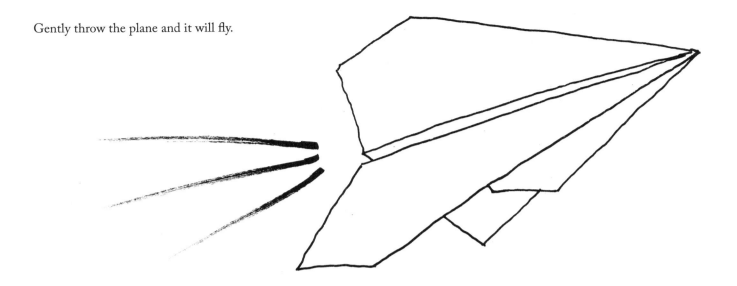

Note down your reflections as you fold.

....

....

....

....

....

....

....

'Where words fail, music speaks.'
Hans Christian Andersen

piano 鋼琴

Music touches our senses. Learning to play an instrument has been shown to improve memory, spatial reasoning, coordination and mathematical ability, reduce stress and also promote happiness, while listening to music affects our moods and emotions. In short, music can be a powerful tool in improving our mental well-being. In the world of music there are many wonderful instruments but I believe that the piano has been the most significant in modern times. Since its invention in the seventeenth century the piano has been central to nearly all genres of music: classical, jazz, pop, soul, dance, hip hop, country, etc.

As you fold your piano, become aware of your senses. Notice how your eyes move across the text and diagrams in this book. Feel the texture of the pages as you turn each one. Look at your hands creasing the paper. Feel the edges of your model. Be conscious of your feet on the floor, your back against the chair and the muscles in your arms as they stretch and contract. Listen to the sound of the folding paper and your breathing. Be mindful of background noises, such as the wind blowing, passing traffic or birdsong. Can you hear a plane flying overhead? If you are in a quiet room meditate on the peace and tranquility of the silence. Try not to explain the sounds you hear – why they are occurring is of no importance, just listen and accept their presence.

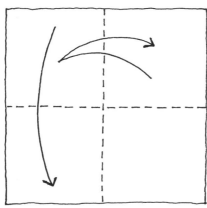

step 1

Valley fold and unfold along the dotted vertical line. Valley fold the horizontal line.

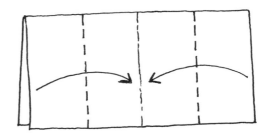

step 2

Valley fold along the dotted vertical lines.

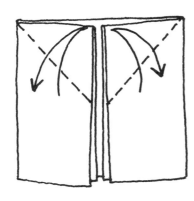

step 3

Valley fold and unfold on the dotted lines.

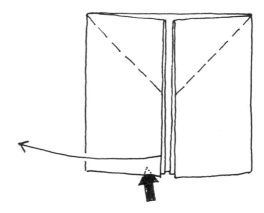

step 4

Open out the top layer indicated by the arrow and fold it down to the left. Repeat on the right side.

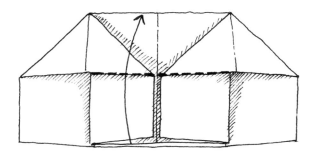

step 5

Valley fold on the dotted line, lifting up the flap.

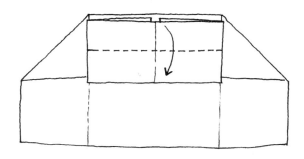

step 6

Valley fold on the dotted line.

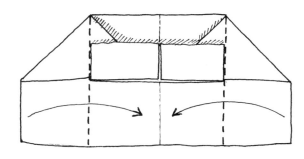

step 7

Valley fold on the vertical dotted lines to make the sides of the piano.

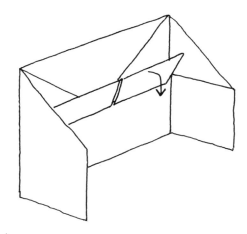

step 8

Fold down the keyboard.

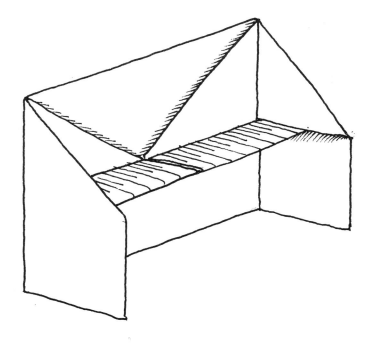

 In origami we fold paper to resemble the shape of animals and objects. But often, to bring the model to life some decoration is required. Adding eyes to an origami animal instantly gives it a character, for example. This model of a piano requires you to draw or paint on it to give it its keys. The pull-out crease pattern at the back of the book already has the keys printed on the paper but if you are using your own paper you will need to draw yours. Why not draw on some pedals and a music stand too?

'Can one achieve harmony with such gentleness by holding on to the true spirit within as if the innocence of an infant?'
Lao Tzu

windmill 風車

Trips to the seaside – building sandcastles, eating ice cream, walking along the waterfront passing shops with brightly coloured windmills spinning in the breeze – these are what cherished childhood moments are made of. Yet at some point that magic, that excitement in those simple joys, fades. At a certain juncture we stop speaking and thinking as children, put away childish things and become adults.

Why is it that as adults we do not share the same sense of wonder in the world as a child? Is it because we cannot, or is it because we choose not to? What would you give to be able to experience the joy and happiness of the world as you did as a child?

One definition of mindfulness is to live in the moment, without judgement. Children live and appreciate the moment and they do not judge, so one way to be more mindful is to be more like a child.

The windmill represents our happiest childhood memories. As you fold its sails, meditate on your most joyful memory – recall the sights, sounds and feelings. Were you with your family or with friends? What were you doing? Feel the emotions of your childhood self; the freedom of having no doubts, concerns or responsibilities.

reflections

One of my childhood memories is my mum singing a Chinese nursery rhyme to me. The song is called 'Roundabout' and the lyrics are about a mother and child experiencing the dragon boat festival. The song opens in a chrysanthemum garden where they are playing on a merry-go-round and eating rice cakes and dumplings. The mother suggests going to see the dragon boats but the child wants to go and see the baby chicks that are being sold at the market. They do go to the market and buy a toy windmill and the final verse recounts the child's joy at how pretty his toy is as it spins.

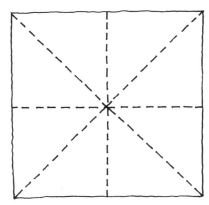

step 1

Start with an opened square base (see page 32).

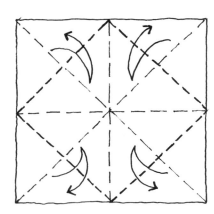

step 2

Valley fold and unfold all four corners into the middle.

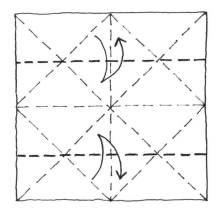

step 3

Valley fold and unfold the top and bottom edges into the middle. Then turn the model by 90 degrees and repeat the folds to give you a 4 x 4 grid of squares.

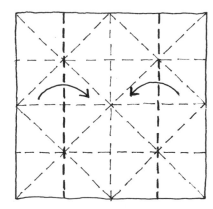

step 4

Now fold the left and right edges back into the middle.

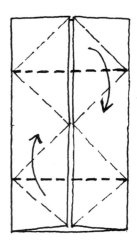

step 5

Valley fold the top and bottom halves so that they meet on the centre line, then unfold them.

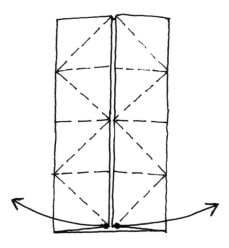

step 6

Pull out both bottom corners and valley fold along the dotted lines.

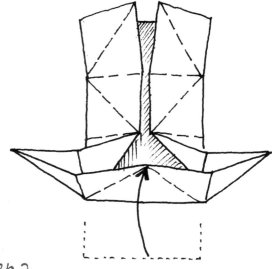

step 7

Flatten the bottom edge. Repeat steps 6 and 7 on the top half of the model.

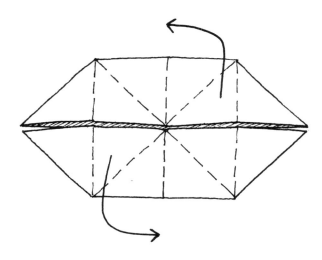

step 8

Valley fold the top right-hand triangle and the bottom-left triangle to form the four arms of the windmill.

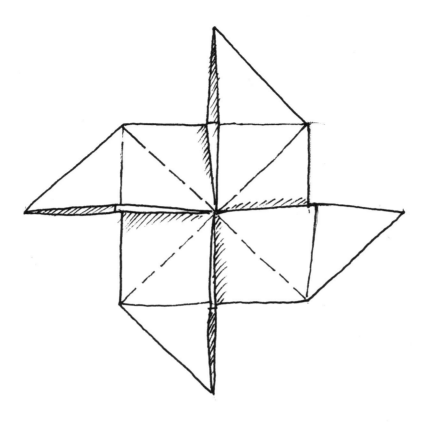

 This is a great model to make with children. Use colourful paper and let them decorate their windmills with glitter by brushing a thin layer of PVA glue on the vanes and then sprinkling over the glitter. You can attach each windmill to a stick with a drawing pin and blow it to spin it. Some of the simplest things can become one of our most treasured memories.

'Study the past, if you would divine the future.'
Confucius

fortune teller 東 南 西 北

Did you play with this model as a child? The fortune teller is a classic playground toy, with fortunes written under its liftable flaps or answers to questions asked of it. Do you remember the first time you saw one? Who was it that folded it? What was the hidden message under the flap?

Wouldn't life be easier if we could see the future? As children we study at school to prepare for it, as adults we work and save money to provide for it. But mindfulness is about living in the present moment; if we can learn to be more mindful in the present our future will be happier.

The theme to reflect on as you fold your fortune teller is therefore the past and the future. Think about a past decision – a good or bad one. Meditate on that decision and consider the thinking behind it. Do not judge yourself – none of us knowingly make a bad decision. We always believe we make the correct decision at that point in time and it is only after the event that the decision can be deemed right or wrong. If you could redo that decision would you have done anything differently?

Or think about a decision that needs to be made. Ask yourself if there is anything in your past that could help you make that decision? Unfortunately we cannot see the future, all we can do is lay the foundations for it. And above all, remember that the future is now; live in the present and make each moment count.

In China this model is called an 'east, south, west, north', as the Chinese version of this game uses the points of a compass, instead of numbers and colours, to indicate which flap to lift. The Chinese translation at the top reflects this name. Fold your fortune teller then see which way the wind blows you…

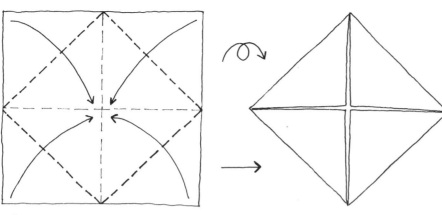

step 1

Start with an opened triangle base (see page 34). Valley fold all four corners into the middle, then turn the model over.

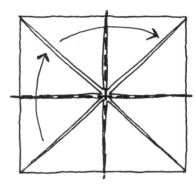

step 3

Valley fold the vertical and horizontal dotted lines. The four corners will come together and collapse into a square base.

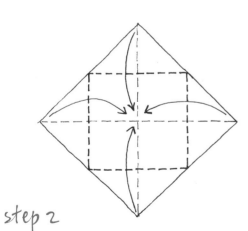

step 2

Valley fold all four corners into the middle.

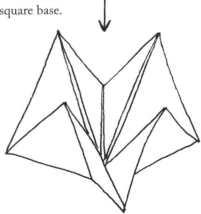

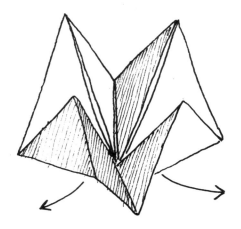

step 4

At the bottom of the model are four corners. Pull each one outwards to complete the fortune teller.

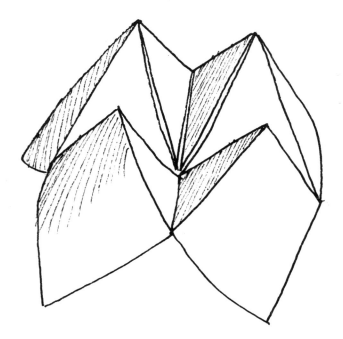

 Use the pull-out crease pattern at the back of the book to annotate your fortune teller. Write four colours on the four outer petals. Write numbers 1–8 on the inner eight triangular faces. Lift each of the number flaps and write a fun fortune in each space. Try 'you will find true love' or 'you will become a rock star'.

'Thousands of candles can be lighted from a single candle, and the life of the candle will not be shortened. Happiness never decreases by being shared.'
Unknown

kite 風箏

The kite is thought to have been invented by the Chinese, though precisely when is not certain. Early models were made from lightweight fabrics, such as silk, and were predominantly used in military circles to carry messages or to measure distances. But as the paper industry boomed, so the paper kite took flight and the kite began to transcend its humble origins and become a toy.

For me, watching somebody fly a kite is a wonderful example of sharing happiness. As an observer, looking up at the brightly coloured object looping and twirling in the sky is mesmerising and enchanting. And if you are the one holding the string you are at play, engaging with a toy and sharing the joy it provides. The simple beauty of holding something in the sky is something everyone should try at least once.

There are moments in our lives when our happiness is shared with others. It might be a spontaneous moment when you have said or done something funny and everyone laughs along with you, or it might be an important event, such as a birthday, a graduation, a wedding or a birth.

Happiness can be contagious – when you are happy, people around you are also happy. Contemplate times when you have passed on your happiness and made others joyful. Today, as you finish folding your kite, share your happiness with everyone around you.

reflections

I have always wanted to write a book on the subject of origami but had never found the motivation. Out of the blue, my Publisher, Liz Gough at Yellow Kite, called me and asked if I would be interested in writing about how origami is mindful. This book is the result of that phone call and I hope to share with you the happiness that origami and that conversation have given me.

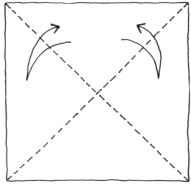

step 1

Valley fold and unfold along the dotted lines.

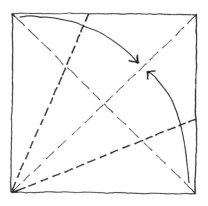

step 2

Valley fold along the dotted lines so that the two edges meet in the middle.

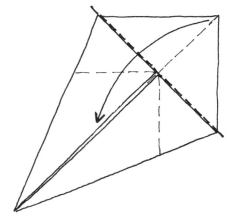

step 3

Valley fold along the dotted line.

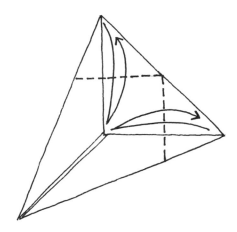

step 4

Valley fold and unfold along the dotted lines (there is a pre-existing crease here). Unfold the model back to an open square and rotate it anticlockwise 45 degrees.

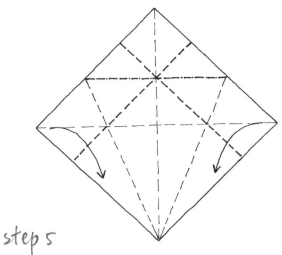

step 5

Note the position of the horizontal mountain fold and the two diagonal valley folds. Make these folds and the model will collapse down like a square base.

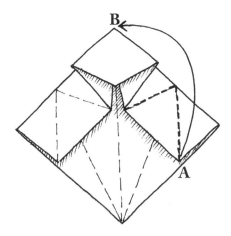

step 6

Note the position of the vertical mountain fold and the diagonal valley folds, then lift the corner point at A and move it to B. Repeat on the left side.

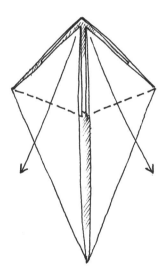

step 7

Valley fold the two flaps along the dotted lines.

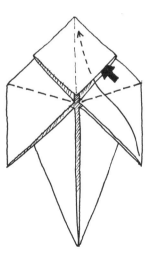

step 8

Open up the top square section as indicated by the arrow. Valley fold along the dotted line, then bend the right triangular flap and tuck it inside the square section. Repeat on the left side. Turn the model over.

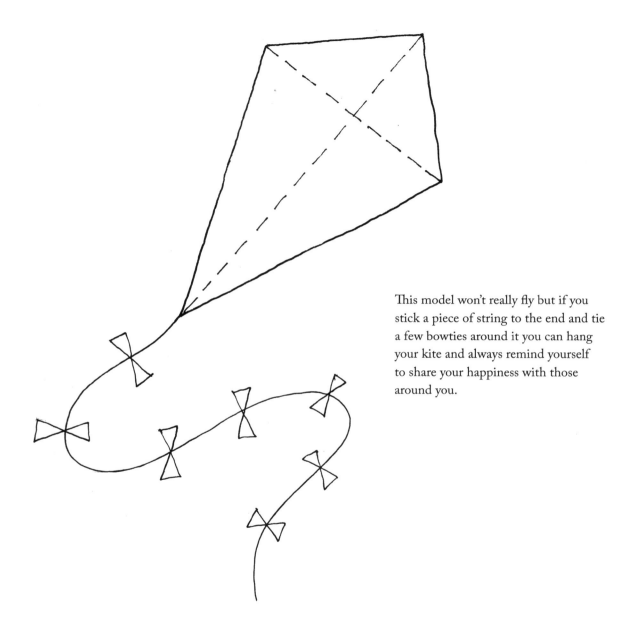

This model won't really fly but if you stick a piece of string to the end and tie a few bowties around it you can hang your kite and always remind yourself to share your happiness with those around you.

'The spirit of the best of men is spotless, like the new lotus in the muddy water which does not adhere to it.'
Buddha

lotus 蓮花

Although all flowers grow in mud, not many grow through mud and water and even fewer have the strength to lift their head above the water line and bloom in the sky. The lotus is a dazzling flower and its beauty appears even more clean and pure when set against a background of dirty, muddy water.

The human spirit is like the lotus – unsullied and uncorrupted – born in the dirty waters of a world full of negativity, greed, lust, hatred and envy. The lotus grows and thrives in the water, yet it blossoms as a pure and untainted flower. This is the aim of mindfulness, to teach you to flourish in a world of negativity, yet to be untouched by its deceitful traits and remain virtuous.

In life we will be confronted by negativity and difficult situations. To be virtuous we have to rise above these and face the situation with a calm and disciplined approach. To be virtuous is to adhere to a code of morality and correct conduct towards others.

As you bend and curl the petals of your lotus flower, meditate on the nature of virtue. One of the main sources of negativity in our life comes from confrontation with others caused by a misunderstanding. Meditate on a time you were able to rise above negativity, when you refused to return the hate directed at you, when you chose to remain calm and de-escalate a potential argument or fight. Our natural instinct is to fight negativity with negativity but instead we should learn to control our thoughts and prevent a confrontation at all. By being mindful of others' feelings we are able to work through disagreements with them and ultimately resolve a misunderstanding without lingering animosity or hatred.

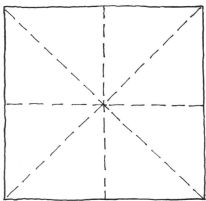

step 1

Start with an opened square base (see page 32).

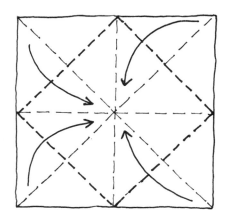

step 2

Valley fold the four corners into the middle.

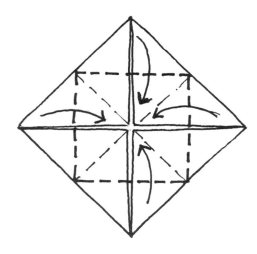

step 3

Valley fold the four corners into the middle.

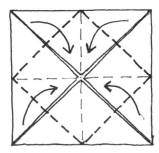

step 4

Valley fold the four corners into the middle, then rotate the model 45 degrees so that it is sitting as a square facing you.

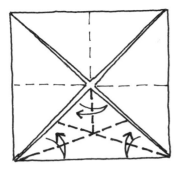 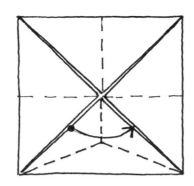 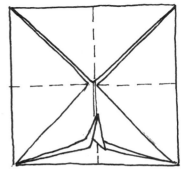

step 5

This step and the next are called a rabbit ear fold. Valley fold and unfold on the dotted lines.

step 6

Pinch the two sides together and it will collapse into the rabbit's ear. Repeat on the other three triangular flaps then turn the model over.

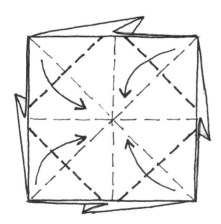 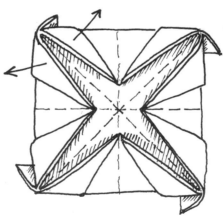 

step 7

Note the positions of the fold lines – they do not form an exact square. Valley fold along the dotted lines. Make the folds through all the layers of the model; this might be a little tricky as it is now quite thick.

step 8

Pull out the fold where indicated to open out a petal. Repeat on the other three corners.

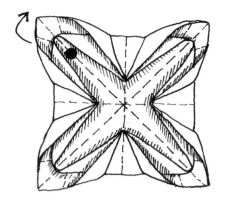

step 9

To complete the shaping of the first layer of petals and give them their natural curved shape, hold your finger down on the spot indicated then slowly and gently pull the corner upwards and curve it round to form a petal – it will be quite stiff but persevere as it will slowly ease round. Repeat on the other three corners. You will find that the base of the model starts to take on a curve like a shallow bowl.

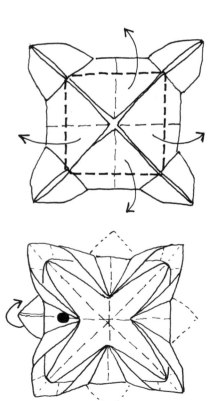

step 10

On the back of the model you will find four corner flaps – these will form the second layer of petals. Pull each corner out and bring them around and over to the front of the model. Hold down on the black spot and pull and curl the corner. Repeat for the other three petals. When you have completed the second layer of petals, you will find the third and final set of corner flaps on the back. Repeat the above step again to form the final set of petals. Please be careful when pulling back the petals as if you pull too hard the paper will tear. You have to gently pull each petal, almost like you are trying to tease it out. You may find that it is easier to wiggle the petal left and right slowly while pulling the petal out. Try to make it with a larger sheet of paper to see if that helps.

Note down your reflections as you fold.

....

....

....

....

....

....

'You have to grow from the inside out. None can teach you, none can make you spiritual. There is no other teacher but your own soul.'
Swami Vivekananda

tulip 鬱 金 香

For centuries flowers have spoken a symbolic language. From the passion of a red rose, to the innocence and purity of a white lily, flowers bear messages of joy, love, remembrance, mourning, peace and friendship.

Tulips find their origins in Persia and Turkey where the delicate bulbs are revered as symbols of fortune, as well as captivating hearts with their enigmatic poise and grace. During the Turkish reign of Ahmed III they were considered such a potent symbol of wealth and prestige that the period later became known as the 'Age of the Tulip'. And when the flamboyant and extravagant plants, with their flame-streaked petals, arrived in Europe, a similar fascination with the flower and its endless mutations and mysteries took hold. In Holland the blooms became the object of a national obsession. Their beauty was so prized that the bulbs took on an almost noble status.

The appearance of the first tulips heralds the start of spring and the reawakening of nature from its winter slumber. As nature begins to bloom and the buds turn to flowers, so we start to think about change and personal development in our own lives. As you fold your tulip, contemplate what you wish to achieve this season. How do you wish to grow as a person? How could you enhance or improve your life in some way or quash any negative aspects of it?

Let your mind wander and contemplate those thoughts and potential changes. By observing our minds we begin to understand and become more aware of ourselves and thus we are better able to control our thoughts and turn them to actions.

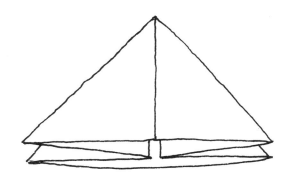

step 1

Start by folding a triangle base (see page 34).

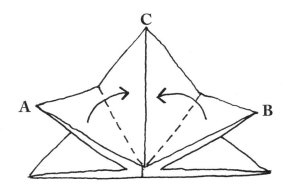

step 2

Working on the top layer only, valley fold A and B up to meet the centre point, C. Turn over and repeat on the other side.

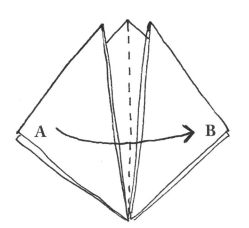

step 3

The next fold is called a 'book turn'. Fold the left side over to the right, as if you were turning back the page of a book. Turn over and repeat on the other side. You should now have a plain square on both sides.

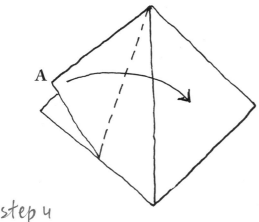

step 4

Valley fold A over the central line by 5mm.

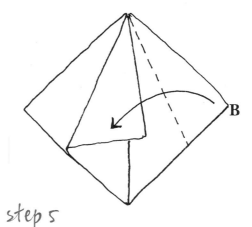

step 5

Do the same on the right-hand side by valley folding B over the central line by 5mm.

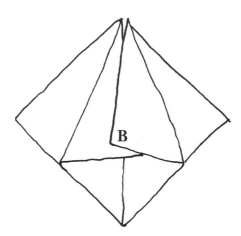

step 6

Turn over and repeat these two folds on the other side.

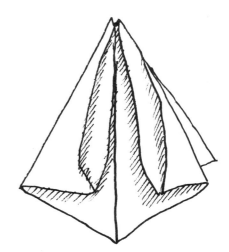

step 7

You now have a kite shape. Open each of the last two folds and you will create a pocket. You are going to force one of the flaps into its opposing pocket.

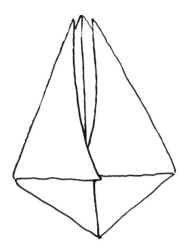

step 8

Push the corner of the right-hand flap into the pocket on the left and force it inside.

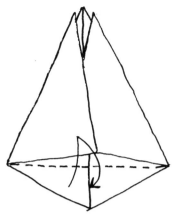

step 9

Valley fold the dotted line and unfold. Turn over and repeat on the other side.

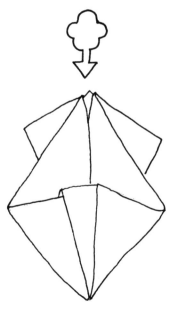

step 10

Rotate the model by 180 degrees and open out the four arms. You will see a small hole in the top. Blow through the hole to inflate the tulip, then gently tap the base to even it out.

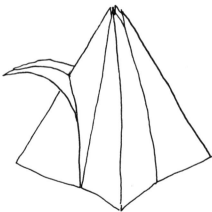

step 11

At the top of the tulip are four corners, which are the tips of the petals. Gently peel each tip back and pull it down, curling it with your fingers. Try to keep the petal shapes symmetrical.

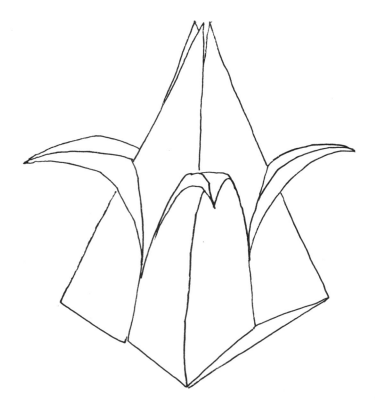

Why not make a bouquet of tulips and give them to someone, or place them in a vase to decorate your house? You can buy green stub wires from garden centres or online and stick them through the centre of the tulips to make stems.

'When you have only two pennies left in the world,
buy a loaf of bread with one, and a lily with the other.'
Chinese proverb

lily 百合花

When I first read the proverb above I didn't think it made sense. Why would a poor man with only two pennies waste one on flowers that could not sustain him? It was only later that I realised that the flower represents spiritual sustenance. The bread will feed his body but the lily will feed his soul.

To live a truly fulfilled life, we need more than material things – we must nourish our hearts and minds as well as our bodies. Many of us are so concerned with fulfilling our material needs that we neglect our mental, emotional and spiritual needs. We are taught that the pursuit of knowledge and academia will lead to successful careers and financial rewards. We rarely consider the acquisition of knowledge to be a pleasurable pursuit yet our minds crave knowledge – you must feed your mind. Every individual will find spiritual sustenance in their own way. Many find it through religion, some find it through the arts, others through sport and travel. Whatever it is it must make us feel like we have a meaningful purpose in life.

As you fold your lily, meditate on what nurtures your soul. It might be reading, cooking or origami, or it might be volunteering for a charity. What makes your heart soar and opens your imagination?

reflections

For a while, origami was just a hobby for me – something I would do on my commute to work. What I hadn't thought about was that I was turning a plain flat piece of paper into something beautiful. Over time origami has become more significant to me; most importantly it has become my daily meditation. As I sit on the train and fold, I contemplate the nature of that model and how it represents facets of me or my life. Origami has also become an unexpected opportunity to talk to strangers. Curious commuters watch me; children ask what I am doing and I usually end up giving them the model. Despite our children growing up in a digital world, it's nice to know that a paper toy will still make them smile.

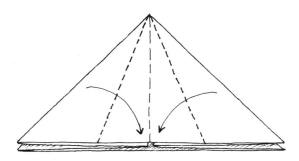

step 1

Start with a triangle base (see page 34). Inside reverse fold along the dotted lines, then turn the model over and repeat on the back.

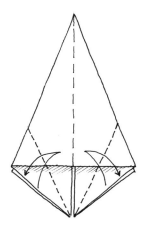

step 2

Valley fold and unfold along the dotted lines. Repeat on the back.

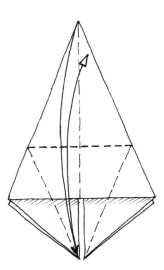

step 3

Valley fold and unfold along the dotted lines through all the layers of the model.

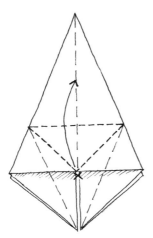

step 4

Note the position of the horizontal
valley fold and the two diagonal mountain folds.
Lift the point X upwards. As you lift you will notice
that the corners A and B will start to move towards
each other. Push A and B together to meet in the
middle. Point X will start to form a triangular point.
Repeat on the other three sides. Please note that this
model is made from a triangle base which has four
branches – you will have to repeat this step four times
in total. Turn the model by 90 degrees and repeat this
step on each branch.

step 5

Valley fold along the dotted line so
that the triangle points downwards.
Repeat on the other three sides, then
rotate the model by 180 degrees.

step 6

Note the triangle flap in the middle of the model.
You are going to make a 'book turn' fold.
Fold just the top layer from left to right, as if you
were turning the page of a book. You will be faced
with a plain diamond shape. Repeat on the back.

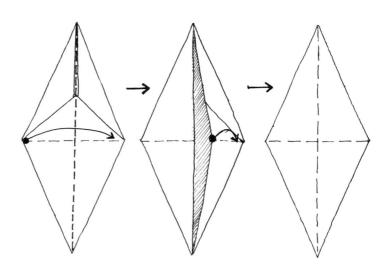

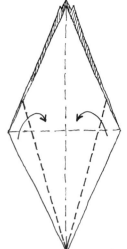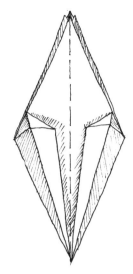

step 7

Taking just the top layer, valley fold along the dotted lines. Repeat on the other 3 sides.

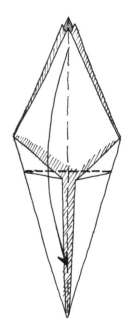

step 8

To create the petals, valley fold along the dotted line, then repeat on the other three sides.

step 9

Gently curl each petal with the back of your finger to complete the lily.

 All flowers make a lovely gift but instead of buying freshly cut flowers as you might normally, why not try making your own bouquet of paper ones for a friend or loved one. A bouquet of origami flowers is also a perfect paper wedding anniversary gift.

'I will write peace on your wings and you will fly all over the world.'
Sadako Sasaki

crane 鶴 鳥

The crane is the most recognised origami model. In Japan the crane represents longevity and is a symbol for peace. Legend has it that if you fold 1000 paper cranes you will have a wish granted. During the Second World War there was a girl called Sadako Sasaki who lived in Hiroshima. On the 6th August 1945 the first atomic bomb was unleashed on Hiroshima's civilian population. Sadako lived through the impact but aged 12 she developed leukaemia. As her health deteriorated she started to fold origami cranes in the hope that after folding 1000 her wish to get well would be granted. As the illness progressed she came to the realisation that she would not get better and she changed her wish to one of world peace. She died after folding 644 cranes but her school friends finished the remaining cranes and buried her with 1000. Sadako's story spread and the Hiroshima Peace Park now has a statue of Sadako holding a paper crane. The inscription below it is: 'This is our cry. This is our prayer. Peace in the world.' Every year on World Peace Day children from around the world send millions of paper cranes to the statue at the peace park as an act of remembrance.

As you fold your crane, meditate on what it means to have peace, not just for your country but for all countries and all peoples. What can you as an individual do to help promote peace in the world for yourself and for those you care for.

reflections

For many years I saw origami purely as a fun but pointless skill. What possible use or good could come from knowing how to fold a paper bird? Then I read the story of Sadako Sasaki. Her story made me realise that something as trivial as a paper bird had given hope to a dying child. That paper bird would later become a symbol for hope and world peace. No matter how trivial and small a thing seems, in a different context it can be deep and meaningful.

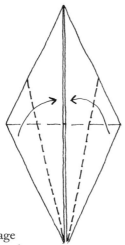

step 1

Start with a bird base (see page 36). Valley fold along the dotted lines, then turn the model over and repeat on the other side.

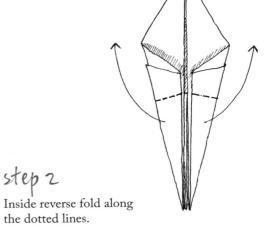

step 2

Inside reverse fold along the dotted lines.

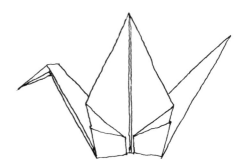

step 3

Inside reverse fold along the dotted line to form the beak.

step 4

Gently pull the wings apart and the body will form.

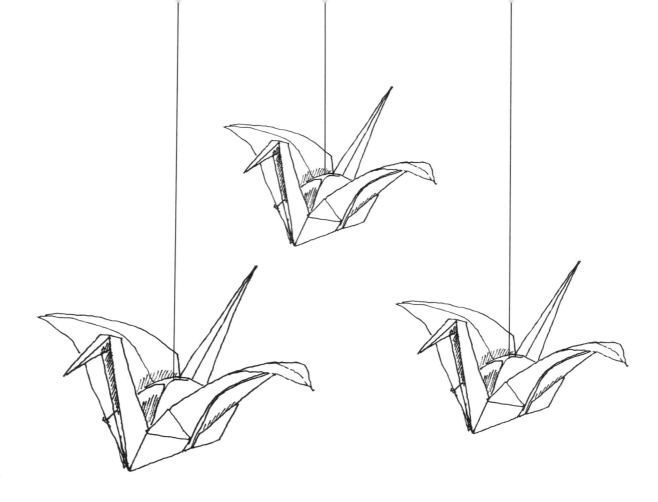

 Why not fold several cranes and make a gift of them? Origami cranes make a beautiful mobile for children. Simply attach your cranes to strings, hang them from wooden sticks or a ring and watch children's eyes light up as the birds fly...

'That which you do not desire, do not do to others.'
Lao Tzu

flapping bird 鳥

The crane and the flapping bird are almost identical models; but while the crane is three-dimensional, the flapping bird is flat. The flapping bird is also one of the rare models that captures not only form but movement in its folds – as its name implies you can pull the bird to make it flap its wings.

Every action has an effect. In all religions and philosophies lies the belief that actions have consequences, both good and bad. In the bible 'a person reaps what they sow', while Buddhism and Hinduism both have the notion of karma: good deeds make the world a happier place whereas bad deeds make it sad.

As you fold your bird and flap its wings, reflect on the nature of karma. What actions have had positive and negative consequences in your life? What can you do to bring yourself good karma, and what deeds might you do to bring more happiness into the world at large?

reflections

The flapping bird is the reason I began folding origami. One of my teachers made a bird and I remember the surprise of my classmates as it started to flap. On my next visit to the library I asked for a book about origami. As a child I was only able to make the simplest models but as I grew I became more confident and progressed to more complex folding. At university I found that origami flowers made great gifts. On a whim, I once advertised a small bouquet I had made on the classified adverts site Gumtree. The bouquet sold and I continued to sell bouquets through the site – until they banned me from doing so! This prompted me to set up my own origami floristry website (www.sesames.co.uk) and sell bouquets myself. For me the positive consequences of that teacher's flapping bird action continue to be felt: it has led to my own business, has allowed me to teach workshops and now to write a book. Where might your next action lead you?

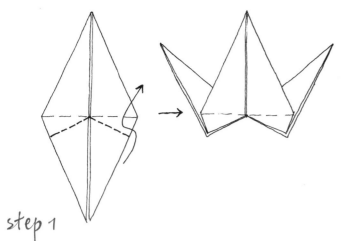

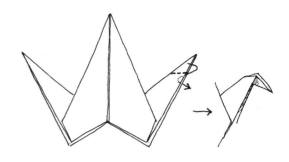

step 1

Start with a bird base (see page 36) with the legs facing downwards. Inside reverse fold along the dotted lines on the top layer, then turn the model over and repeat on the other side.

step 2

Inside reverse fold on the dotted line to form the beak.

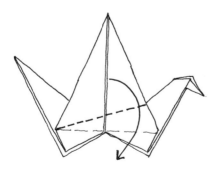

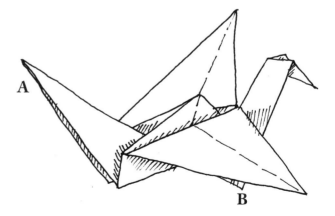

step 3

Valley fold along the dotted line to form the wing, then repeat for the other wing.

To make the wings flap, hold the tail (A) with one hand and the chest (B) with the other and pull the tail downwards to the horizontal position. Pull the tail backwards and forwards and the wings will flap.

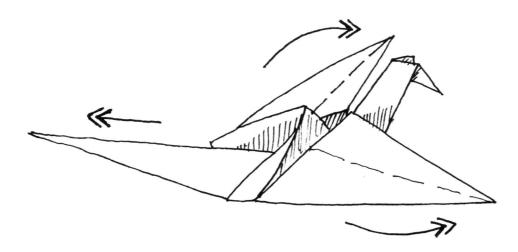

Note down your reflections as you fold.

....

....

....

....

....

....

....

'Love is not when someone else's happiness is more important than your own. It is when someone else's happiness is your happiness.'
Samuel Tsang

heart

To live, your heart must beat, but to be truly alive you need more than blood pumping through your heart – you need it to be filled with love. Our mind may control our thoughts and reasoning but our heart is where we feel love.

Love can take many forms. Of course there is romantic love and love for our family, but there is also love for life itself and all that it may bring; a life with this kind is essential for feeling fulfilled. The love of our family is what raises us to be good people and, when we are ready, we want to give that love to others and raise our own families.

As you fold your origami heart, think of someone you love who makes you smile from inside. Feel the warmth of the thought of that person and send them your feelings. Then reflect and feel their love as it is sent back to you and wrapped around you.

reflections

What does love mean to you? I have spent years searching for a definition of love and one of the best I came across was the quote above. But I feel the English word 'love' is often misunderstood and used in the wrong context. One should not speak of love lightly. I much prefer the way the Ancient Greek language defines love; they have several words for it:

agape – love of humanity or of God (this is the highest form of love)
eros – romantic love
philia – love of a friend
storge – love for a parent or child

Who are the people you love? The people I love are my mother, father, sister, wife and children and these people can be described in one word: family.

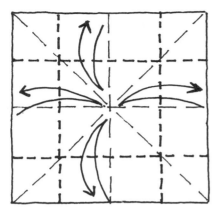

step 1

Start with an opened triangle base (see page 34).
Valley fold and unfold on the dotted lines.

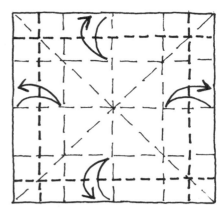

step 2

Valley fold and unfold along the dotted lines.

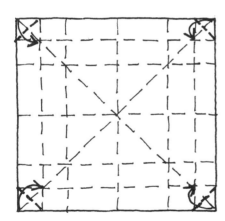

step 3

Valley fold the four corners on the dotted lines.

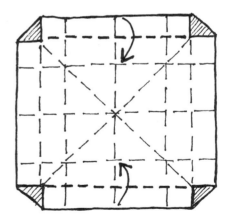

step 4

Valley fold along the dotted lines.

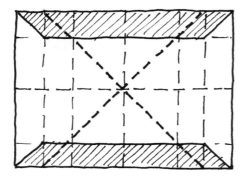

step 5

Note the horizontal mountain fold and the two diagonal valley folds and collapse the model like a triangle base.

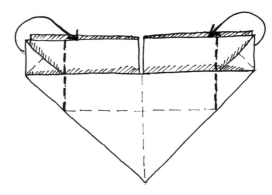

step 6

Mountain fold on the dotted line and repeat on the back.

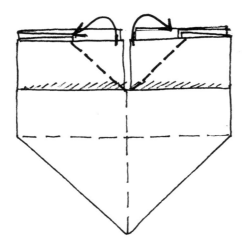

step 7

Inside reverse fold on the dotted lines.

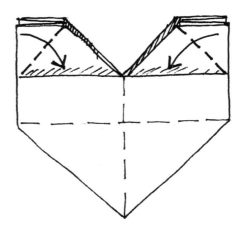

step 8

Valley fold along the dotted lines and repeat on the back.

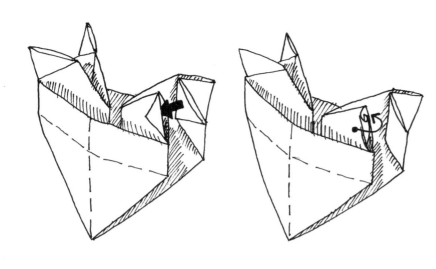

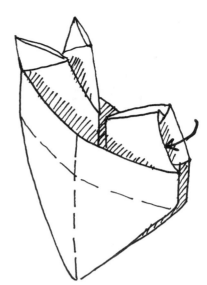

step 9

Focusing just on the top right-hand corner of the heart, turn the model towards you and look at the edge. There will be a pocket as shown by the arrow. Open this pocket up slightly. Bend and roll the front triangular flap and tuck it into the pocket, then tuck the back triangular flap into the same pocket. You will find that this locks the right side of the heart. Repeat step 9 on the other side.

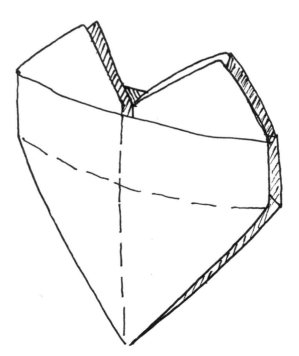

'An elephant never forgets.'
Unknown

elephant 象

Memories are what make us who we are – they are our past but can also shape and influence our future. Elephants have an impressive memory and this has been scientifically proven. Studies show that they can remember water and food sources in a vast territory and are able to navigate to them during times of drought and famine. They are able to recognise other elephants – and humans – that they have met decades after their last meeting. And they also recall where their tribal burial grounds are and always try to return there with dying members of their herd.

So it follows that the theme to reflect on as you fold your elephant is remembrance – specifically, remembering the people that have helped you along your way in life. Naturally our family and friends will be dominant in our lives but there are many others that have crossed our paths and may have had a lasting impact on our actions, views and our understanding of the world – people such as our teachers, work supervisors, religious leaders, gym instructor or even our origami teacher. Think about the people that have helped you or changed your life in some way and be grateful for the role they have played.

reflections

I created this elephant model in 2014 after I received an email from Jordan Christmas at ZSL Whipsnade Zoo. She contacted me to ask if I would like to help in trying to beat the world record for the largest number of origami elephants ever displayed. The zoo wanted to raise awareness of the endangered status of elephants. They wanted to have 30,000 models, which is the estimated number of elephants left in the wild. I accepted and in turn sent an email out to all the members of the British Origami Society asking for help. Over the next few months people from all over the world started posting hundreds of origami elephants to the zoo. In October, myself and three other members of the British Origami Society spent eight hours counting origami elephants. Our final count was 33,768 and ZSL Whipsnade Zoo was officially awarded the world record for the largest display of origami elephants. The paper elephants are still a permanent exhibit. This was an origami adventure I will never forget!

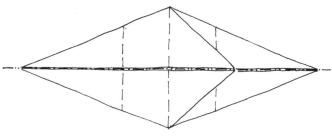

step 1

The elephant model has a lot of outside and inside reverse folds (see page 25) so you need to be confident with them before beginning this model. Start with a fish base (see page 38). Mountain fold along the dotted line.

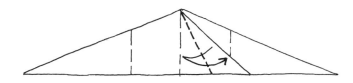

step 2

Valley fold and unfold along the dotted line, then repeat on the back. Please note that for steps 2–6 when you turn the model over the triangular flap you are folding will be the reflection of the above illustration. Just make the fold in the same way to mirror the illustration.

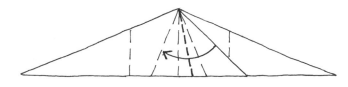

step 3

Valley fold along the dotted line, then repeat on the back.

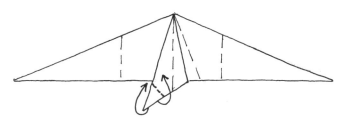

step 4

Outside reverse fold along the dotted line. You will need to open up the side of the model to achieve this (see page 27). Repeat on the back.

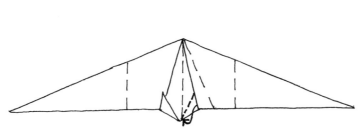

step 5

Inside reverse fold along the dotted line. Note that the inside reverse fold is folded through both layers of the leg. Repeat on the back.

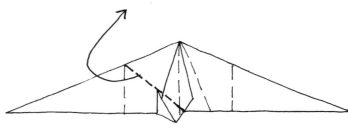

step 6

Inside reverse fold along the dotted line. Please note that this reverse fold is made through all the layers of the model. Also note that the dotted line starts from the middle of the model and runs to the top of the crease line one third in from the left; you will have to move the leg out of the way to make the initial valley fold crease.

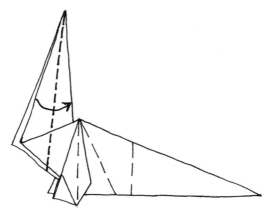

step 7

Valley fold along the dotted line and repeat on the back.

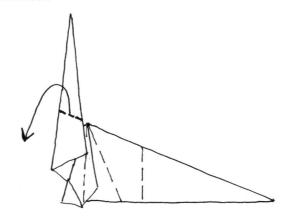

step 8

Inside reverse fold along the dotted line (you are starting to fold the elephant's trunk).

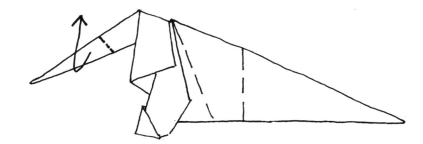

step 9

Inside reverse fold along the dotted line. Steps 9–11
will complete the shaping of the trunk – don't worry
about making the angles identical to the images in
the illustrations; you can make the trunk point in any
direction you like.

step 10

Inside reverse fold along the dotted lines to complete
the trunk.

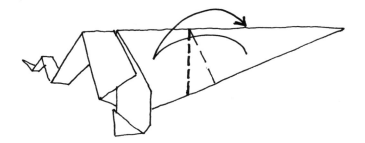

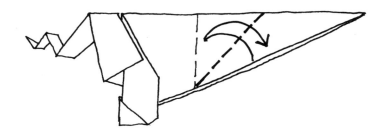

step 11

Rotate the model anticlockwise slightly so that the
back is straight. Valley fold and unfold along the
dotted line.

step 12

Valley fold and unfold along the dotted line.

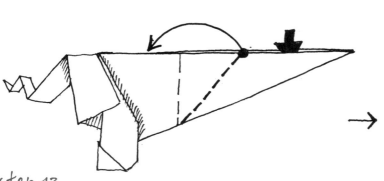

step 13

Open up the back of the model. Note the position of the valley and the mountain fold on the body, then lift up the tail, push down and flatten it.

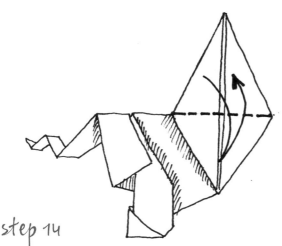

step 14

Valley fold and unfold along the dotted line.

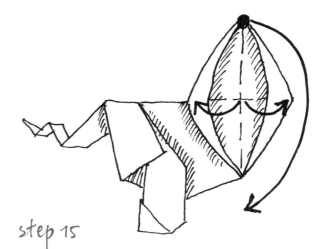

step 15

Pull open the tail and fold the tip at the top downwards.

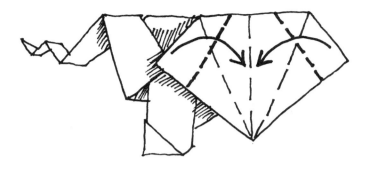

step 16

Valley fold along the dotted lines so that the edges meet in the middle.

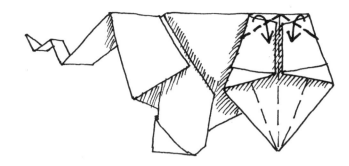

step 17

Valley fold along the dotted lines so that the edges meet in the middle.

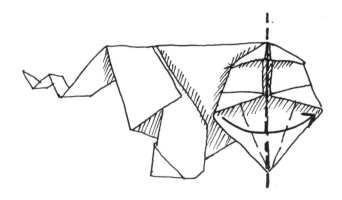

step 18

Valley fold along the dotted line to bring the back together.

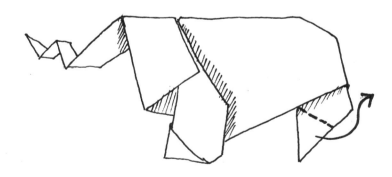

step 19

Inside reverse fold along the dotted line to form the back foot and a small tail.

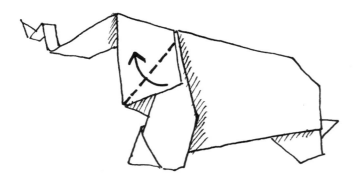

Valley fold on the dotted line to form the ear.
Repeat on the other side.

Note down your reflections as you fold.

....

....

....

....

....

....

....

'To support mother and father, to cherish wife and children, and to be engaged in peaceful occupation – this is the greatest blessing.'
Buddha

squirrel 松鼠

There is a family of squirrels that lives in my back garden. Every morning I see them running back and forth along my garden fence collecting their food. In spring, baby squirrels appear and my daughters and I watch them grow. In autumn we look on in admiration as they bury their food to prepare for the winter months. I find it inspiring how the squirrels work together to support themselves and to raise their family.

As your paper squirrel takes shape, reflect on the last time you derived some satisfaction from your work or were happy about the completion of it. Remember the feeling and sensation when you first accepted that offer and the excitement of learning new things and meeting new people. Do you have a good work–life balance? Can you do anything to even the weight? If your work is a source of anxiety or disappointment, think back to tasks that gave you satisfaction. How can you regain that feeling?

reflections

I designed this squirrel model for my youngest daughter, Remy. When I think of Remy I see her holding her milk bottle with both hands like a squirrel grasps a nut. Recalling that memory warms my heart and clears my mind of any negative thoughts.

The squirrel is the most complex model in this book. You will need to have completed all the other models before attempting to fold your squirrel. Use paper with a coloured and a white side, fold your model slowly, make sharp folds and check each step carefully.

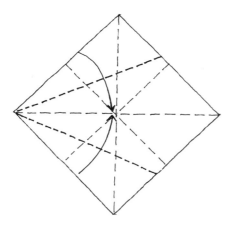

step 1

Start with an open square base (see page 32) with the
white side of the paper facing you. Valley fold along
the dotted lines so that the edges meet on the central
line.

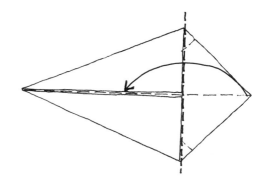

step 2

Valley fold along the dotted line.

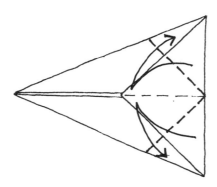

step 3

Valley fold and unfold on the dotted lines (the
corners will meet in the middle). Now unfold
the paper back to the open square base in step 1.

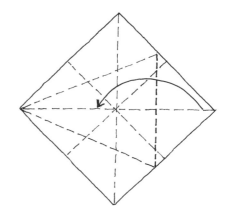

step 4

Valley fold along the dotted line.

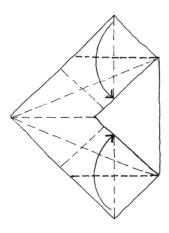

step 5

Valley fold and unfold on the dotted lines, then fold
back to the kite in step 2.

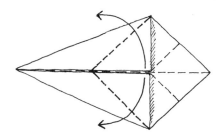

step 6

Valley fold along the dotted lines.

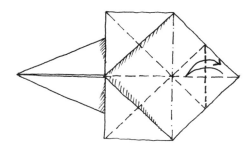

step 7

Valley fold and unfold along the dotted line.

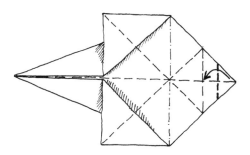

step 8

Valley fold and unfold along the dotted line.

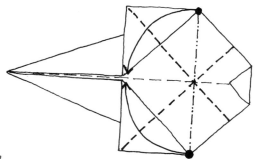 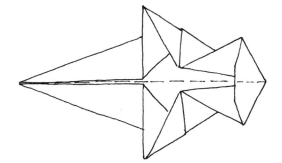

step 9

Note the positions of the two diagonal valley folds and the vertical mountain fold. As you fold the two points to meet in the centre the white area will collapse like a triangle base. Rotate the model anticlockwise by 90 degrees.

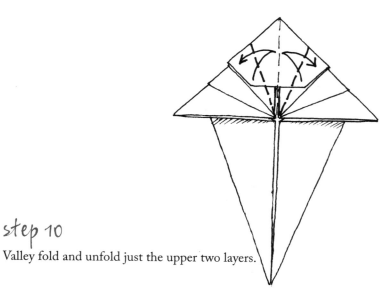

step 10

Valley fold and unfold just the upper two layers.

step 11

Note the position of the horizontal valley fold and the two diagonal mountain folds. Petal fold (see page 37) along the dotted lines.

step 12

Fold and unfold a rabbit ear on the dotted lines (see page 71).

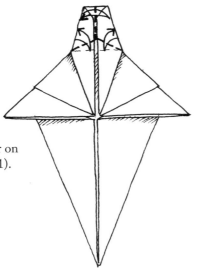

step 13

Open up the section of the model indicated.

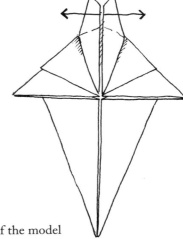

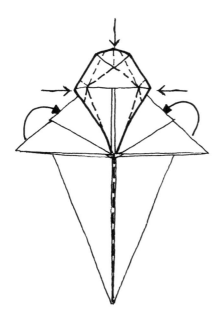

step 14

The next few steps are the most difficult in this book. First mountain fold the arm and tail sections backwards and hold them together in one hand. Now focus only on the head section.

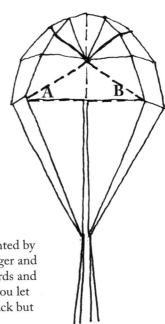

step 15

Focus on the triangle highlighted by the heavy line. Using your finger and thumb push A and B backwards and pinch them together. When you let go the model might spring back but this is perfectly fine.

step 16

The head should look a little like a cobra's head in its ready-to-strike position. Pinch together at the point indicated by the arrows. Note the two valley folds inside the head – when you pinch at this point the two sides will collapse down.

step 17

Move your fingers further up and again pinch your fingers together at the point indicated by the arrows.

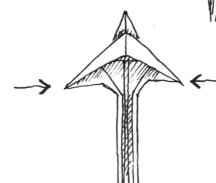

step 18

Use your fingers to pinch the sides of the head together to flatten it, then turn the model on to its side.

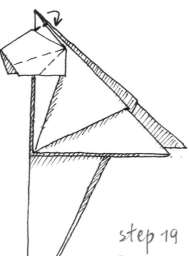

step 19

Inside reverse fold along the dotted lines to form the ears.

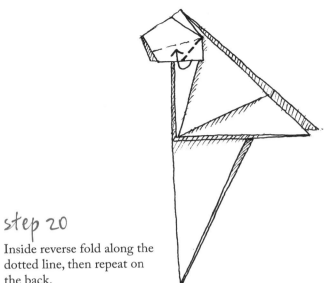

step 20

Inside reverse fold along the dotted line, then repeat on the back.

step 21

Valley fold along the dotted line, then repeat on the back.

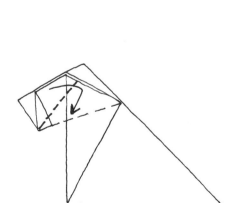

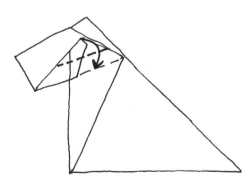

step 22

Valley fold along the dotted line, and repeat on the back.

step 23

Valley fold along the dotted line, and repeat on the back.

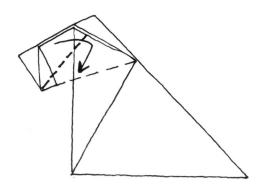

step 24

Valley fold along the dotted line and repeat on the back.

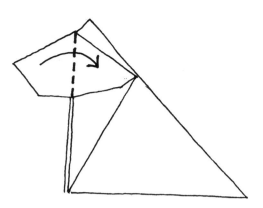

step 25

Valley fold and unfold along the dotted line.

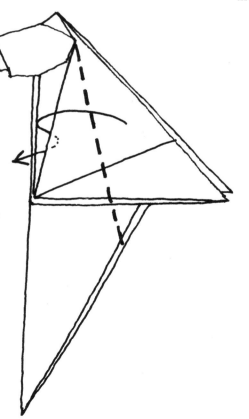

step 26

Inside reverse fold along the dotted line and repeat on the back.

step 27

Valley fold and unfold,
then repeat on the other side.

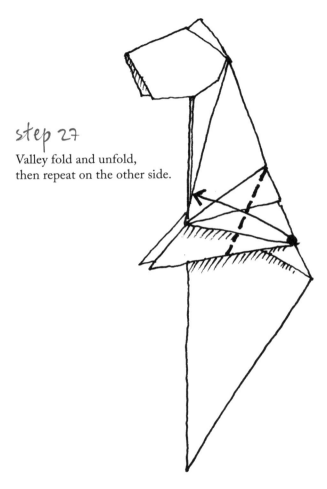

step 28

Inside reverse fold on the
dotted line and repeat on
the other side.

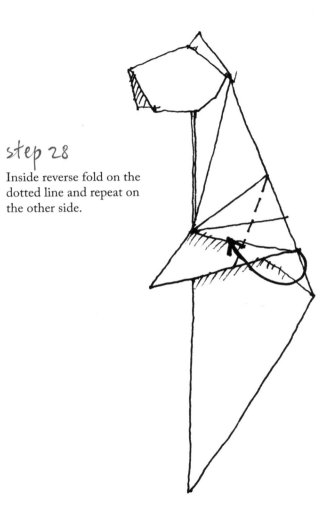

step 30

Open the model at the point indicated by the arrow. Note the position of the valley fold that was created in the previous step. Start to lift the corner tip (indicated by the dot) upwards – you only need to lift the very top layer. Lift it upwards and over, pivoting on the horizontal valley fold. Move the tip so that it is below the chin of the squirrel. Repeat on the other side.

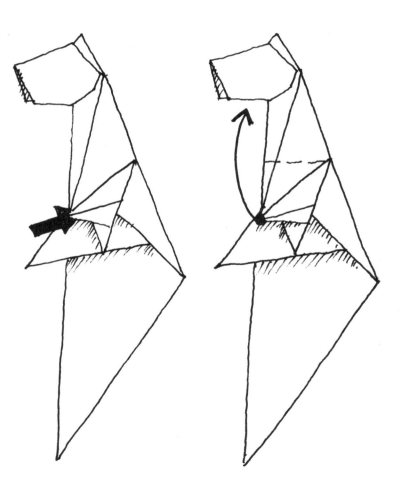

step 29

Valley fold and unfold along the dotted line through the entire model.

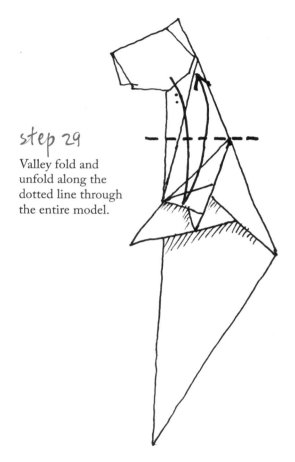

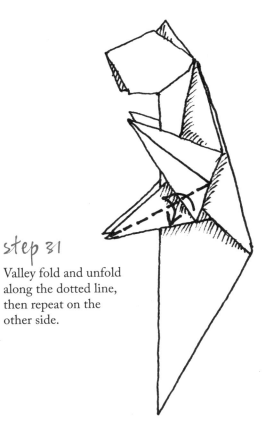

step 31

Valley fold and unfold
along the dotted line,
then repeat on the
other side.

step 32

Valley fold just the upper layer of
paper along the dotted line. As
you make the fold the point A will
swivel to meet the edge of the foot
at B. Repeat on the other side.

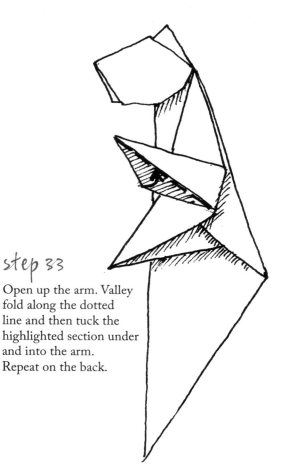

step 33

Open up the arm. Valley fold along the dotted line and then tuck the highlighted section under and into the arm. Repeat on the back.

step 34

Valley fold along the dotted line and then tuck the highlighted section under into the arm. Repeat on the back.

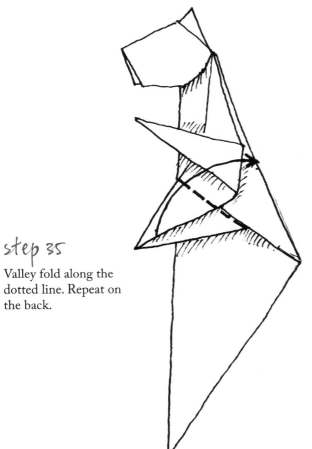

step 35

Valley fold along the
dotted line. Repeat on
the back.

step 36

Valley fold along the dotted line.
Repeat on the back. Now unfold
both legs back to step 34.

step 37

Crimp fold (see page 28) on the dotted lines to form the foot and repeat on the back. Note the position of the valley fold and the mountain fold. A crimp fold is two inside reverse folds, one fold inside of the other. Make the first inside reverse on the valley fold so that the foot is tucked inside of the body. Then make a second inside reverse on the mountain fold so that the toe is now facing outwards.

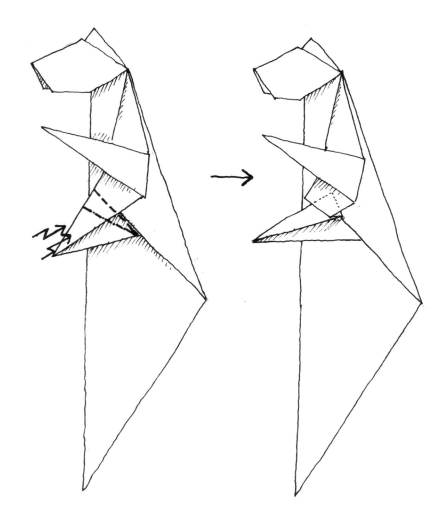

step 38

To make the tail, open up the back of the model. Pull the tail backwards and up – this results in an inside reverse fold along the dotted line.

step 39

Valley fold along the dotted line and repeat on the back.

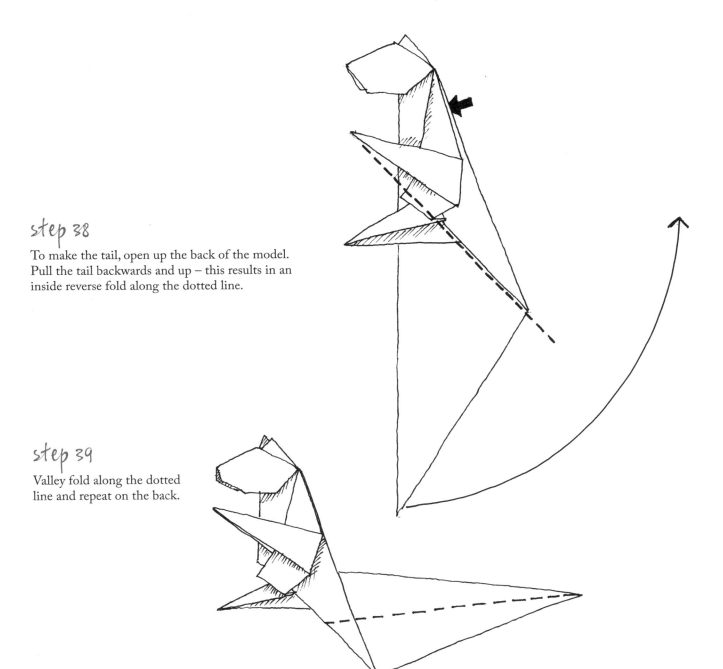

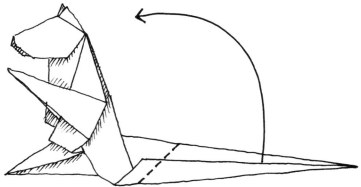

step 40

Outside reverse fold along the dotted line.

step 41

To finish the squirrel, push a little on the nose
and the head will round out. Use your fingers or
a pen to give the tail a curl.

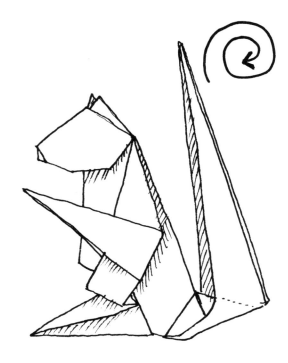

'Knowing others is intelligence; knowing yourself is true wisdom. Mastering others is strength; mastering yourself is true power.'
Lao Tzu

self 自我

You have reached the final chapter of this book. Thank you for reading the stories, making the models and meditating on their themes. I hope that you have experienced the calm and therapeutic qualities of origami.

The final model is you. The theme will be yourself and the model you make will symbolise you.

There are two ways to approach this final model. Firstly, meditate on yourself. Meditate on who you are and what type of person you would like to be. What animal or object do you believe represents the values you hold? This will become your model and in turn, your totem.

Your model can be anything – a bird, an animal, a flower, a vehicle or an object that you feel an affinity with. Once you have decided on that totem try to find an origami diagram of it and learn to fold it. If you cannot find an existing model try and create one yourself.

The second approach, and the one I recommend, is just to fold without a shape or form in mind and see what you end up with. When you finish folding, your model might vaguely resemble something. If this happens continue folding and see if you can make it resemble that form more. I believe that this second path is traditionally how most origami models were created. If you choose this method you will truly be creating.

reflections

Which model did I choose for myself? I chose an origami crane. I like the symbolism of being a blank piece of flat paper that has been transformed into three-dimensional object form through my own efforts. And with that I wish you all the best for your own origami journey.

further reading

Below is a list of websites I hope you will find useful for finding out more about origami and mindfulness. If you have any questions or comments you can find me on all social media portals @mindFOLDness #mindFOLDness

general

www.mindfulorigami.com
My website for this book where you can download crease patterns and find more information about the book. (@mindfulorigami #mindfulorigami)

www.mindfoldness.com
Focussing on developing the concepts behind mindFOLDness, the site allows you to discuss and share your models, coloured crease patterns and meditations. (@mindFOLDness #mindFOLDness)

origami

British origami society: **www.britishorigami.info**
This is a useful starting point to learn more about origami.

Origami USA: **www.origamiusa.org**
An American website with diagrams and information.

Lang origami: **www.langorigami.com**
The origami website of Dr Robert Lang, who has been a student of origami for over 40 years and is now recognised as one of the masters of the craft. It has impressive examples of advanced origami models and explains the use of origami in science and medicine.

mindfulness

www.mindful.org
A site whose purpose is to inform, inspire, guide, and connect all those who want to live a mindful life, and to create a more mindful and caring society.

bemindful.co.uk
The Mental Health Foundation's guide to how mindfulness can help us all have a healthier, happier life.

www.nhs.uk/conditions/stress-anxiety-depression/pages/mindfulness.aspx
The UK's NHS page about mindfulness.

www.headspace.com
A popular mindfulness app for smartphones and tablets.

This book is dedicated to the two funniest people I know – Cammy and Remy. It is for when you are old enough to read and fold. If you are ever stuck and don't know what to do, ask me, I will always be there. Love Baba xx

Origami was an idle pastime for me until my wonderful wife Carmen said, 'you should go and teach some workshops'. That piece of advice started the ball rolling on my origami career and has taken me on some of my most interesting adventures. I thought organising the world record for the largest display of origami elephants was to be the highlight of my origami career but no, it turns out it is this book. This book is a direct consequence of the love and encouragement from the most amazing person I know. I love you, Carmen.

Thanks to my parents, Yun Kwai Tsang and Ka Tsun Tsang for just about everything. Thank you for all the love, wisdom and knowledge you have given me and for always being there. With special thanks to my dad for supplying the Chinese calligraphy too. Thanks to my sisters Susan and Sandra for their support and encouragement.

I would like to thank my good friend Kat Osman (Director of Lick PR) who was my first ever origami customer; she purchased 20 stellated octahedron for the release of the video game Fear Effect II back in 2001.

Thanks to Mily Quan and Pui Fong Leung for helping to test-fold my origami models, and also Toshiko Kurata for supporting me in teaching origami workshops.

Thanks to Elise Wong and Ellen Wong for being my mindfulness advisers; to Jo Nhan for being my yoga adviser, and Vee Charununsiri for his in-depth knowledge of Indian and African elephants.

Thanks to all my friends who have chosen to stay by my side over the years and for all the late-night discussions about life, love, food, existence, science, philosophy, religion, champagne, Goldie's teeth, Louboutin shoes and chocolate buttons.

Thanks to my publisher, Liz Gough, for finding me and giving me this amazing opportunity to fulfil a life ambition. And special praise for my amazing book team, who produced such a wonderful book in such a short time: Imogen Fortes, my editor, for giving warmth and grace to my words; Lucy Gowans, for making this book beautiful, and Richard Neal for his equally beautiful illustrations. And finally I would like to thank all the staff at Yellow Kite who have helped create, support and promote this book.

First published in Great Britain in 2016 by Yellow Kite
An imprint of Hodder & Stoughton
An Hachette UK company

Text copyright © Samuel Tsang 2016
Illustrations copyright © Richard Neal 2016
Calligraphy copyright © Ka-Tsun Tsang 2016

The right of Samuel Tsang to be identified as the Author of the Work has been asserted by him in accordance with the Copyright, Designs and Patents Act 1988.

A CIP catalogue record for this title is available from the British Library

Trade Paperback ISBN 978 1 473 63501 2

Publisher: **Liz Gough**
Design: **Lucy Gowans**
Illustrations: **Richard Neal**
Project editor: **Imogen Fortes**
Chinese calligraphy: **Ka-Tsun Tsang**

Printed in Spain by EstellaPrint

Hodder & Stoughton policy is to use papers that are natural, renewable and recyclable products and made from wood grown in sustainable forests. The logging and manufacturing processes are expected to conform to the environmental regulations of the country of origin.

Hodder & Stoughton Ltd
Carmelite House
50 Victoria Embankment
London
EC4Y 0DZ

www.hodder.co.uk

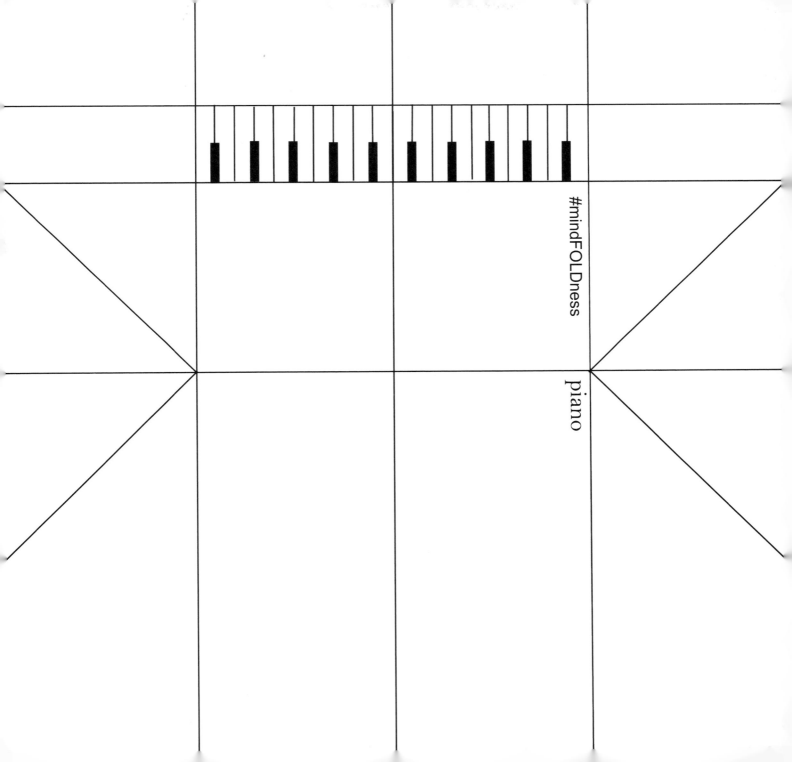

#mindFOLDness

piano

piano

fortune teller

#mindFOLDness

fortune teller

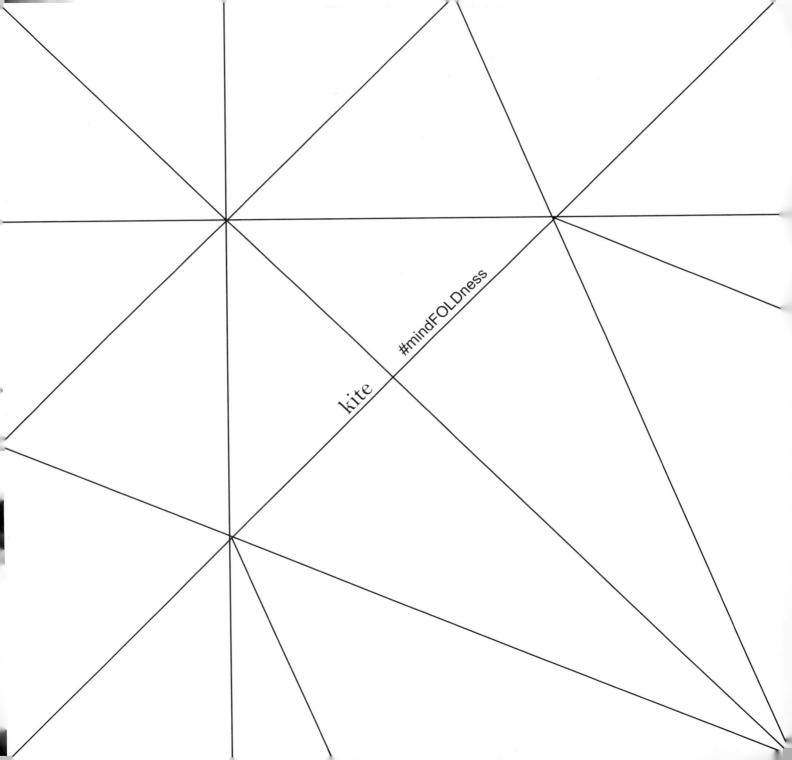

kite #mindFOLDness

kite

lotus

蓮花

lotus

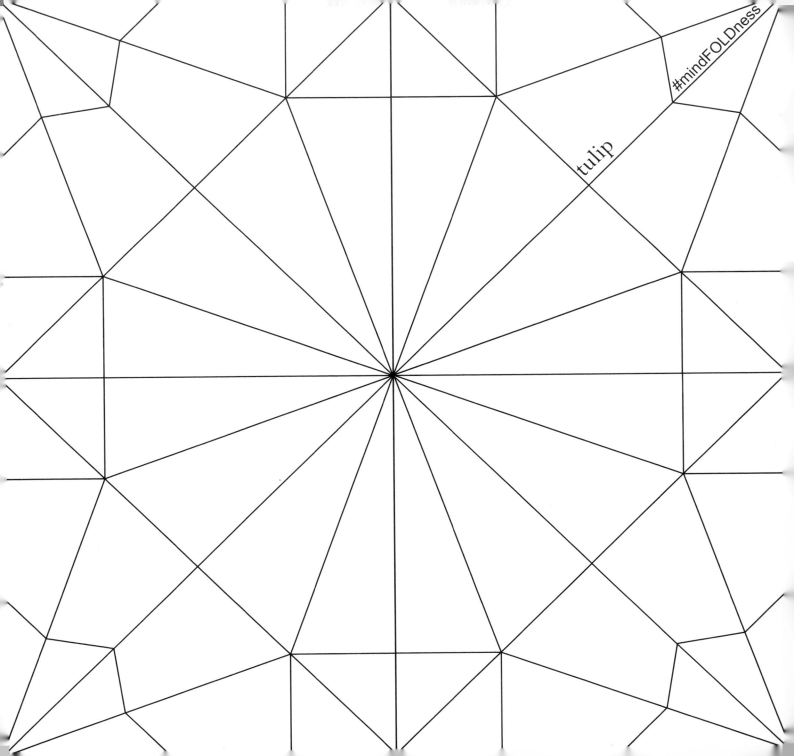

tulip

#mindFOLDness

tulip

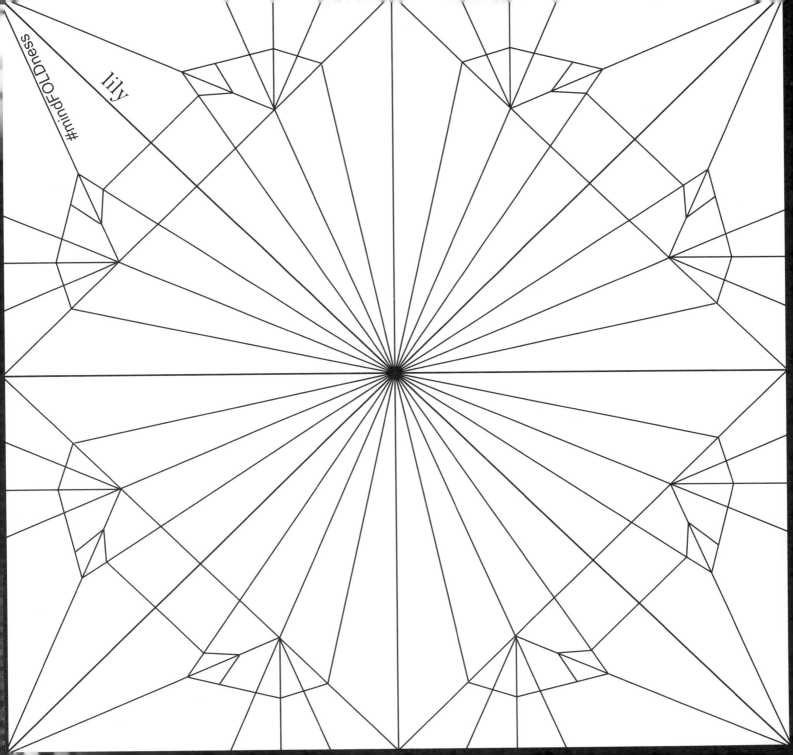

lily

#mindFOLDness

lily

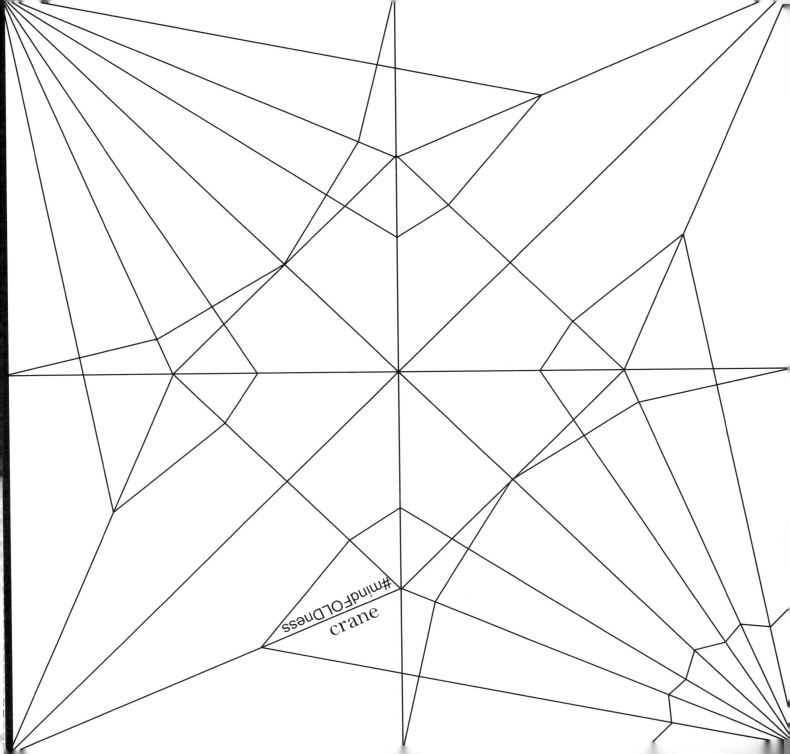

crane
#mindFOLDness

crane

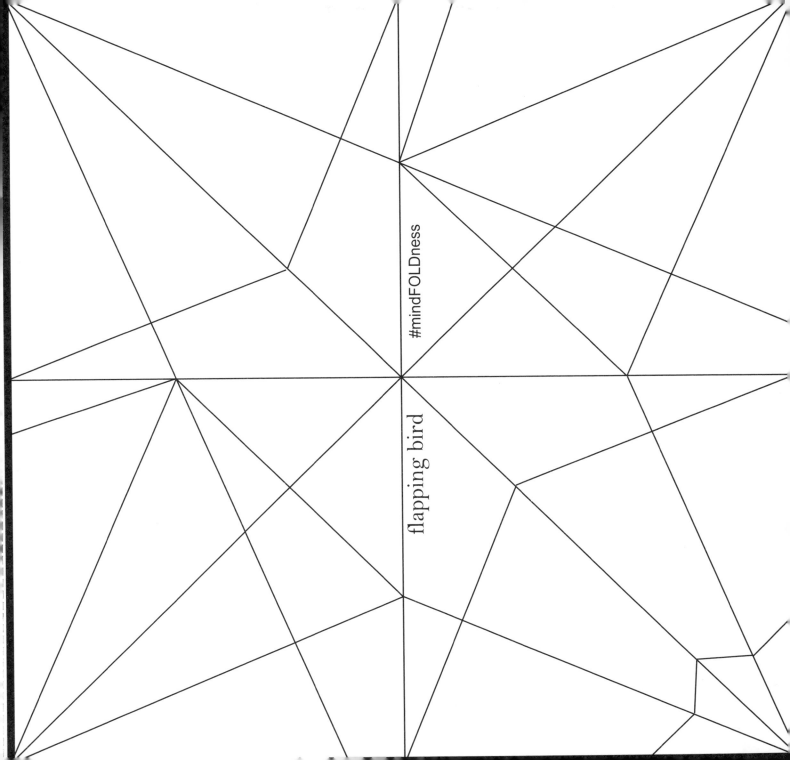

#mindFOLDness

flapping bird

flapping bird

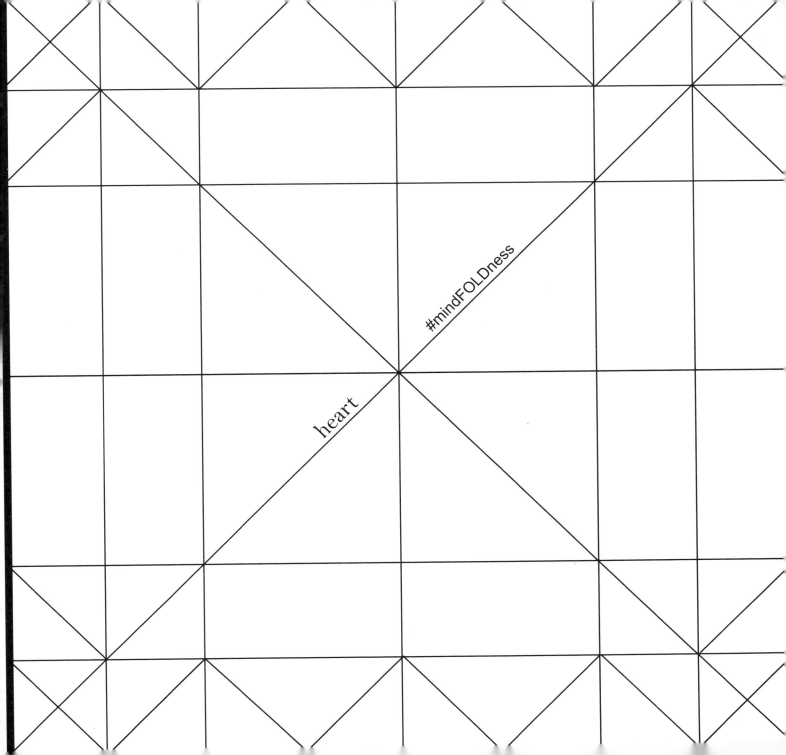

heart

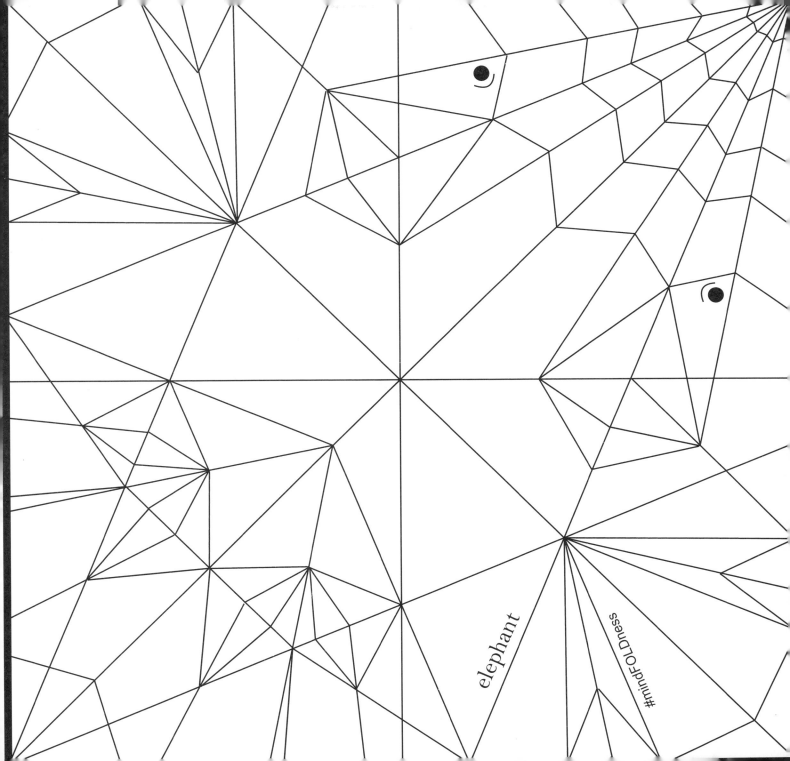

elephant

#mindFOLDness

elephant

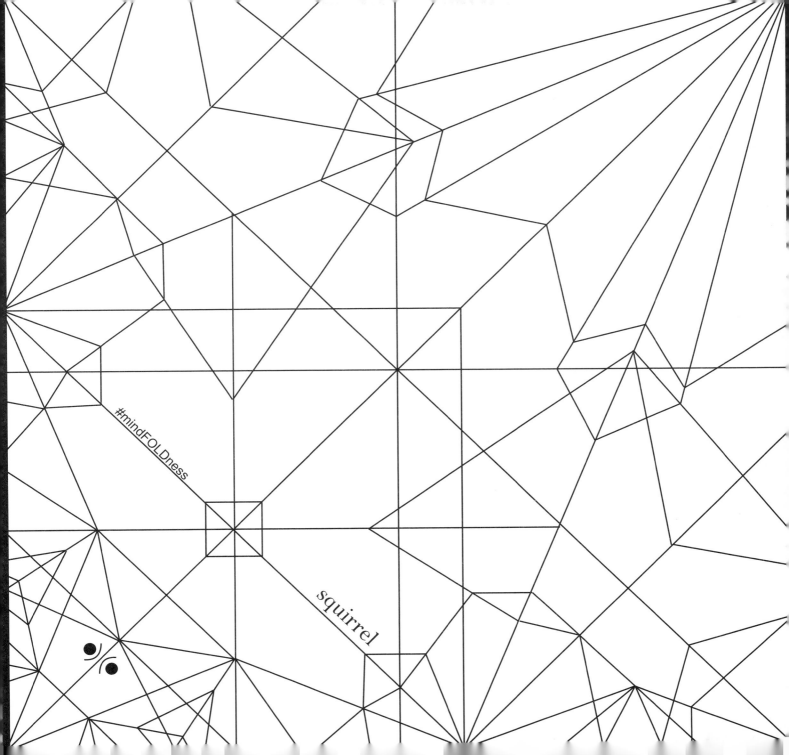

#mindFOLDness

squirrel

squirrel

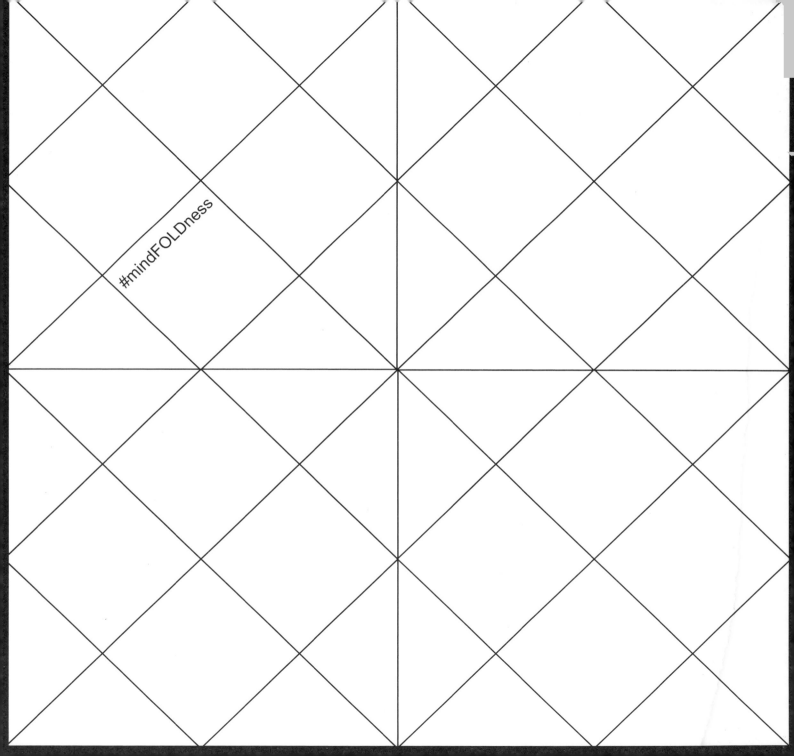
#mindFOLDness

make of it what you will